Longman Practice Exam Papers

GCSE Physics

Keith Palfreyman

LONGMAN

Series editors

Geoff Black and Stuart Wall

Titles available for GCSE

Biology
Chemistry
Mathematics (Intermediate)
Mathematics (Higher)
Physics
Science

Addison Wesley Longman Ltd, Edinburgh Gate, Harlow, CM20 2JE, England
and Associated Companies throughout the World

© Addison Wesley Longman 1998

All rights reserved; no part of this publication may be reproduced, stored in a retrieval system, or transmitted in any form or by any means, electronic, mechanical, photocopying, recording or otherwise without either the prior written consent of the Publishers or a licence permitting restricted copying in the United Kingdom issued by the Copyright Licensing Agency Ltd, 90 Tottenham Court Road, London, W1P 9HE.

First published 1998

ISBN 0 582 35648 2

British Library Cataloguing-in-Publication Data
A catalogue record for this book is available from the British Library.

Set in 11/13pt Times

Printed in Great Britain by Henry Ling Ltd, at The Dorset Press, Dorchester, Dorset.

Contents

Editors' preface   iv

Acknowledgements   iv

How to use this book   1

Paper 1 – Foundation and Higher   3

Paper 2 – Foundation and Higher   21

Paper 3 – Foundation and Higher   37

Solutions to practice exam papers   46

How well did you do?   63

Editors' Preface

Longman Practice Exam Papers are written by experienced GCSE examiners and teachers. They will provide you with an ideal opportunity to practice under exam-type conditions before your actual school or college mocks or before the GCSE examination itself. As well as becoming familiar with the vital skill of pacing yourself through a whole exam paper, you can check your answers against examiner solutions and mark-schemes to assess the level you have reached.

Longman Practice Exam Papers can be used alongside the *Longman GCSE Study Guides* and *Longman Exam Practice Kits* to provide a comprehensive range of home study support as you prepare to take your GCSE in each subject covered.

Acknowledgements

As always, I am indebted to colleagues and friends for their patience and advice. In this case the staff of the Science department of Pope Pius X and the pupils there were as helpful and supportive as ever and their knowledge and comments were welcome. My son Paul again found time to check the manuscript for me and found the errors and made relevant suggestions with his usual thoroughness. My wife, Angela, put up with yet another spate of frantic keyboard pounding and without her the task would have been so much more difficult.

Finally thanks to Geoff Black, Stuart Wall, Linda Marsh and all of the people at Longman without whom these books are impossible.

KEITH PALFREYMAN

How to use this book

What's it all about?

Mock examinations are an extremely important part of your final GCSE year. In some courses the examinations will be before Christmas and in others they will be planned for January or February. In either case the examinations are there for a number of reasons, including the following:

- *To give you a realistic idea of your progress.* The result should give you a fair idea of your progress and what sort of result you are capable of getting in the final examination. You may find out that you can do better than you expected, or that you need to do much more revision and make a greater all round effort. In either case it is important that you do your best at this stage so that you can make realistic decisions about what you need to do in the following term. Do remember that you will not have completed all of the coursework at this stage and that your result in the final examination will be correspondingly better. Most students improve their mock examination grades by at least one grade in the final examination.

- *To help decide the level of your entry for GCSE.* After the examination you and your teacher will need to decide whether you will be entered for the Foundation level or Higher level at GCSE. The mock exam will usually be done under examination conditions in the same hall, etc., as your final GCSE and therefore gives a good idea of how you are likely to perform under exam conditions. This is very different from doing homework assignments or working in class, and the extra pressures can sometimes make a big difference. Some people are able to work well under exam conditions but others, although just as intelligent, find it harder. It is important that you are entered for the correct level so that you get the highest possible grade in the end and the mock exam provides valuable evidence to help with this.

- *To give you experience of working under examination conditions.* Doing a whole set of mock examinations in formal examination conditions is not the same as doing class tests or end of year exams. There is a lot more pressure and more rules that have to be obeyed. It is important that you experience this before the 'real thing' so that you will know what to expect and can cope with it better. Treat the mock examinations as you will the final exams and it will help you to gain confidence.

- *Estimated grades.* Your teacher will have to send to the Examination Board a list of the grades that all the students are expected to achieve in each subject. Your mock examination result will be used to help to arrive at this grade.

- *Special consideration.* If you are seriously ill or have an accident that prevents you from taking the final examination, then it may be that your school will ask for you to be awarded a grade under the Special Consideration scheme. The Examination Board will need evidence to be able to do this and, as part of this evidence, they will usually ask for your mock examination paper. Your school will usually keep your mock examination paper for that reason – but do keep it yourself if it is returned to you. This paper will not be very useful under these circumstances unless you did your best in the examination!

Using these practice exam papers

There are three examination papers designed to try to help you with your revision at this important stage. You should attempt them in the allocated time so that you can use the results to improve your marks in the school mock exams and in the GCSE exam itself.

All of the papers have questions on a range of different topic areas and you should be able to attempt most questions by this stage. If you find that there is work that you have not yet covered, do your best to pick up as many marks as possible. Sometimes it helps to leave such questions until the end. If you are good at the other questions you may have more time then to work out your best answers.

- Make sure that you have done enough revision for the practice examination to be a fair test.
- Choose a suitable time. Look at the length of the examination paper and make sure that you can do it in one session. The third paper is shorter than the other two, so this is one that you can do when time is short.
- Choose a suitable place. You will need somewhere where you will not be disturbed by others – parents bringing a drink or friends arriving are not helpful here!
- Have all the materials that you might need – pen, pencil, ruler, calculator – as you will for the real GCSE examination.
- Start on time. Read the instructions on the papers carefully, especially about the level of the questions. Higher level questions are marked *** and you can leave them out if you are only wanting to do the Foundation/Basic level paper.
- If you are doing the Higher level questions, allow the extra time that is suggested.
- End on time. Use any spare time to check your answers for errors or work missed out.
- DON'T CHEAT – the answers are there, but you need to find out how good you are! If you find that you are totally unprepared, do some more revision and try again on another day.
- If you are doing the Foundation Tier questions and you found the examination easy, give yourself the extra time that is stated on the front of the paper and see how well you can do with the Higher Tier questions.
- Mark your answers. The answers are all in the section later in the book, together with tips on how you might improve your answers and some possible alternatives. Again it is important not to cheat. Mark the work fairly so that YOU know how well you have done. There is no reason why you should mark the work immediately after doing it. Sometimes it is better to wait so that you have more time to learn from the tips. The total marks are given in the solutions section so that you can assess your progress.

List of formulae

You may use the following equations and information in the tests if you need to do so.

$$\text{Density} = \frac{\text{mass}}{\text{volume}}$$

Gravitational field strength at the earth's surface = 10 newtons per kilogram

Weight = mass × gravitational field strength $\quad W = m \times g$

Electric power = potential difference × current $\quad P = V \times I$

$$\text{Efficiency of a system} = \frac{\text{useful output energy}}{\text{total input energy}}$$

For a transformer: $\dfrac{\text{secondary voltage}}{\text{primary voltage}} = \dfrac{\text{number of turns on secondary coil}}{\text{number of turns on primary coil}}$

Longman Examination Board

General Certificate of Secondary Education
Physics
Paper 1

Foundation

Time: 1 hour 30 minutes

Instructions

- For the Foundation Tier paper you should do all of the questions *except* those marked ***.
- Answer the questions in the spaces provided.

Higher

Time: 1 hour 45 minutes

Instructions

- For the Higher Tier paper you should do all of the questions *including* those marked ***.
- Answer the questions in the spaces provided.

Name ....

There is a list of formulae that you may use on page 2.

Number	Mark
1.	
2.	
3.	
4.	
5.	
6.	
7.	
8.	
9.	
10.	

---

1. (a) The diagram shows how a hydroelectric power station can be used to generate electricity.

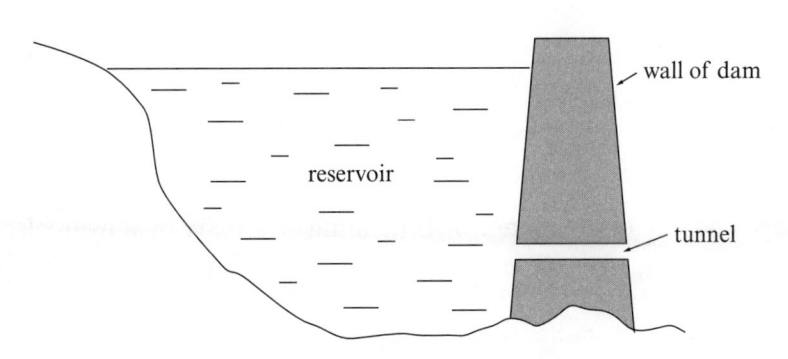

Leave margin blank

A turbine/generator is placed in a tunnel in the wall of the dam.

Turn over

(i) Put an arrow on the diagram to show which way the water flows though the turbine/generator. **(1 mark)**

(ii) As the water passes through the turbine/generator it has kinetic energy. What do we call the energy in the water in the reservoir behind the dam?

....

(1 mark)

(iii) What is the main energy transformation that takes place inside the turbine/generator?

....

....

(2 marks)

(iv) This process does not convert all of the energy contained in the water into the form that we want. Explain why.

....

....

....

....

(2 marks)

(b) Hydroelectricity is an example of a **renewable energy resource**.

(i) Explain what is meant by a renewable energy resource.

....

....

(2 marks)

(ii) State the names of **two** other renewable energy resources.

1. .... **(1 mark)**

2. .... **(1 mark)**

(iii) Some energy resources are **non-renewable**.
State the names of two non-renewable energy resources.

1. .... **(1 mark)**

2. .... **(1 mark)**

(c) All sources of energy have advantages and disadvantages.

(i) Give one advantage and one disadvantage of generating electricity by a hydroelectric power station.

Advantage..

.... **(1 mark)**

Disadvantage..

.... **(1 mark)**

(ii) Give a reason why a country might choose to use one of the **non-renewable** energy resources that you named. (Make sure that your answer shows which of the resources you are discussing.) Now do the same for one of the **renewable** energy resources that you named.

....

....

(2 marks)

(d) Electricity is a **secondary energy resource** because the energy must first be transformed from another energy resource. The original resource is called a **primary energy resource**. State **two** advantages that electricity has for users when compared with using a primary energy resource.

1. ....

.... **(1 mark)**

2. ....

.... **(1 mark)**

Total: 18 marks

2. The diagram shows a number of different circuits. All the circuits use the same kind of batteries and bulbs. All the bulbs are lit.

Circuit 1

Circuit 2

Circuit 3

Circuit 4

(a) (i) Which bulb will be brightest?

....

(1 mark)

Turn over

(ii) Explain why this bulb is the brightest.

....

....

(1 mark)

(b) In which circuit does the battery supply the smallest current?

....

(1 mark)

(c) Copy circuit 2 into this space and add to your diagram a meter that will measure the current through bulb D.

(2 marks)

(d) In circuit 3, someone opens the switch S. Complete the following table to show whether the bulbs are on or off.

Bulb	On or off
E	
F	
G	

(3 marks)
Total: 8 marks

3. The 13 amp plug in the diagram was connected to a small microwave oven. When it was opened it appeared as shown below.

(a) State two mistakes that were made when the plug was wired.

1. ....

....

2. ....

....

(2 marks)

(b) What is the fuse for?

....

....

(1 mark)

(c) Use these equations to answer the following question.

Units of electricity = power × time

Cost of electricity = energy transferred × cost per unit

The panel on the back of the microwave oven says that it has a power rating of 0.9 kW. In one week it was used for 5 hours. The cost of electrical energy is 8p per kilowatt-hour. What was the cost of using the oven during that week?

....

....

....

(2 marks)

(d) Some appliances have only two wires connected in the plug.
  (i) Which two wires are connected?

  1. .... 2. ....   **(2 marks)**

  (ii) When it is safe to connect an appliance in this way it will be **double insulated**. Explain what this means.

  ....

  ....

  ....

  (1 mark)

  (iii) An appliance that is double insulated will have a special symbol marked on it. Draw this symbol in the space below.

  (1 mark)

*** (e) In a modern house, a 13 amp plug will be plugged into a socket on a **ring main**.
  (i) Explain, with a diagram if you think it helps, what is meant by a ring main.

  ....

  ....

  ....

  (1 mark)

  (ii) Explain the advantages of using a ring main.

  ....

  ....

  (2 marks)

Turn over

*** (f) The electricity in a 'mains' circuit in a house is a.c.
  (i) What does a.c. stand for?

  ....
  (1 mark)

  (ii) How is a.c. different from the current that is supplied by batteries?

  ....

  ....

  ....
  (1 mark)
  Foundation Tier – Total: 9 marks
  Higher Tier – Total: 14 marks

4. A new train is being tested along a straight track.
   Its speed is recorded every 20 seconds. The results are shown on the graph below.

   (a) Describe the motion of the train in sections BC and CD of the graph.

   ....

   ....

   ....
   (2 marks)

   (b) (i) How far does the train travel in part BC?

       ....

       ....
       (1 mark)

(ii) How far does the train travel in part AB?

....

....

....

(2 marks)

(c) Calculate the acceleration of the train in the first 20 seconds shown on the graph.

....

....

(2 marks)

(d) (i) Write down the equation that links force with mass and acceleration.

....

(1 mark)

(ii) The train has a mass of 20 000 kg.
Use your equation to calculate the force produced by the train in the first 20 seconds.

....

....

....

(2 marks)

(e) The train has a lot of kinetic energy between points B and C.
What happens to this energy as the train is braked to a stop in the time it travels from C to D?

....

....

(1 mark)

*** (f) Calculate the kinetic energy of the train in the section BC.

....

....

....

(3 marks)

Turn over

*** (g) Trains are usually prevented from crashing by keeping the track in front clear, so they do not have the same sort of collisions as cars. At the end of the line there are buffers that the train will hit if it does not stop in time. Using your knowledge of forces, acceleration and energy explain why these buffers will contain large springs rather than just being solid.

....

....

....

....

(3 marks)
Foundation Tier – Total: 11 marks
Higher Tier – Total: 17 marks

5. (a) Give one use for each of the following waves:

   (i) microwaves .... **(1 mark)**

   (ii) ultra-violet .... **(1 mark)**

   (iii) infra-red .... **(1 mark)**

   (iv) ultrasound .... **(1 mark)**

   (b) (i) Which of the waves in (a) has the greatest frequency? ....

   (1 mark)

   (ii) Which of the waves in (a) has the greatest wavelength? ....

   (1 mark)

   (iii) Which of the waves in (a) will have the slowest speed in air? ....

   (1 mark)

   (c) When you listen to a sound wave, its frequency and its amplitude will have a big effect on what you hear.
   (i) What will you hear if the frequency of the sound is increased?

   ....

   (1 mark)

   (ii) What will you hear if the amplitude is made smaller?

   ....

   (1 mark)

   (d) (i) Write down the formula which connects the speed of a wave with its frequency and its wavelength.

   ....

   (1 mark)

(ii) A water ripple travelling across the surface of a pond has a wavelength of 25 cm and a frequency of 5 Hz. What is the speed of the ripple across the surface?

....

....

Speed = ... cm/s **(1 mark)**

(e) A family live in a house which is close to the new runway of an airport.
Name two things that the family could do to reduce the noise caused by the aircraft.

1. .... **(1 mark)**

2. .... **(1 mark)**

(f) Some factories and other work-places are very noisy. One example of this is on farms where the tractor drivers have to work in very noisy cabs.

(i) What problems can be caused by working in noisy places?

....
(1 mark)

(ii) How can the tractor driver make the effects of the noise less serious?

....
(1 mark)

(iii) The loudness of the sound can be measured by using a special meter.
What units would be used for the measurements?
.... **(1 mark)**

Total: 16 marks

6. (a) A scientist stands a Geiger tube in the middle of his test bench and connects it to an electronic counter. He finds that it is recording 80 counts per minute even though he has not brought a radioactive source into the room.

(i) What is this count called? .... **(1 mark)**

(ii) Where does this radiation come from? ....

.... **(2 marks)**

Turn over

(b) The scientist then collects a radioactive source from his safe and moves the Geiger tube towards it. He finds that the count rate begins to increase when he is a few centimetres or so from the source and then it gets higher as he moves even nearer to the source. When the source is close to the detector the scientist puts a piece of thick paper between them and the count rate falls to 80 per minute again.

  (i) What sort of radioactivity is being emitted by the source?

  ....

  (1 mark)

  (ii) It must be possible for any other person to know that the safe contains a radioactive source.
  The diagram below shows 5 different hazard symbols.

  A   B   C   D   E

  Which of the symbols will be shown on the door of the safe? .... **(1 mark)**

  (iii) As well as keeping the source in a safe, the scientist must take other precautions. Name two other things that he must always do when he wishes to experiment safely with the radioactive source.

  1. .... **(1 mark)**

  2. .... **(1 mark)**

(c) Some radioactive sources emit gamma radiation.
  (i) In what way is this radiation different from both alpha and beta radiation?

  ....

  ....

  (1 mark)

  (ii) Name a use for gamma radiation.

  .... **(1 mark)**

(d) Another scientist has been asked to design a machine to check the thickness of thin aluminium foil as it is made at a factory.

(i) Which type of radioactivity will be suitable for this machine? ....

(1 mark)

Explain your answer.

....

....

.... **(1 mark)**

(ii) What will the scientist do to make sure that the radiation only travels in the direction of the detector?

....

....

(1 mark)

*** (iii) The scientist will also need to check the **half-life** of the material that he chooses to use in the machine. Explain what is meant by half-life and why it is important in this case.

....

....

....

....

(2 marks)

*** (e) Strontium 90 is a radioactive material which emits beta particles.
This is shown by the following equation.

$$^{90}_{A}Sr \longrightarrow ^{0}_{-1}\beta + ^{B}_{39}Y$$

Use the equation to work out

(i) the atomic number A (proton number) of strontium .... **(1 mark)**

(ii) the atomic mass number B (nucleon number) of the new atom Y .... **(1 mark)**

Foundation Tier – Total: 12 marks
Higher Tier – Total: 16 marks

7. (a) John has cut a long strip of polythene from a plastic bag.
He rubs this on his sleeve and hangs it over his pencil.
He is surprised to see the two parts of the strip move apart as shown on the diagram.

His older sister explains to him that the plastic has a static electric charge.
(i) Why do the strips of plastic move apart?

....

(1 mark)

Turn over

(ii) John then puts his hand between the two strips. What do you expect will happen?

....

(1 mark)

(iii) John rubs the strip again so that the two parts repel as before. He then rubs his pen, which is made of plastic, on his sleeve in the same way as he did the strip and puts it between the two parts of the strip. Explain what happens.

....

....

(2 marks)

(iv) Explain carefully how the charge got on to the strip when John rubbed it on his sleeve.

....

....

....

....

(2 marks)

(b) A gardener is spraying insecticide on to plants in a large greenhouse.
The insecticide goes though a small hole as it leaves the spray gun and is broken up into tiny droplets. There is a small electric charge on each droplet.
Explain how this charge helps to make the insecticide cover the plants better.

....

....

(2 marks)

(c) John's father is repairing a computer and tells him that the same sort of static electric charge can damage the chips inside the machine. What can his father do to make sure that the chips are not damaged in this way?

....

....

(1 mark)
Total: 9 marks

Leave margin blank

8. (a) A student switches on a light box which makes a narrow beam of light. She points the beam across a piece of white paper so that it hits a strip of mirror at an angle, as shown in the diagram.

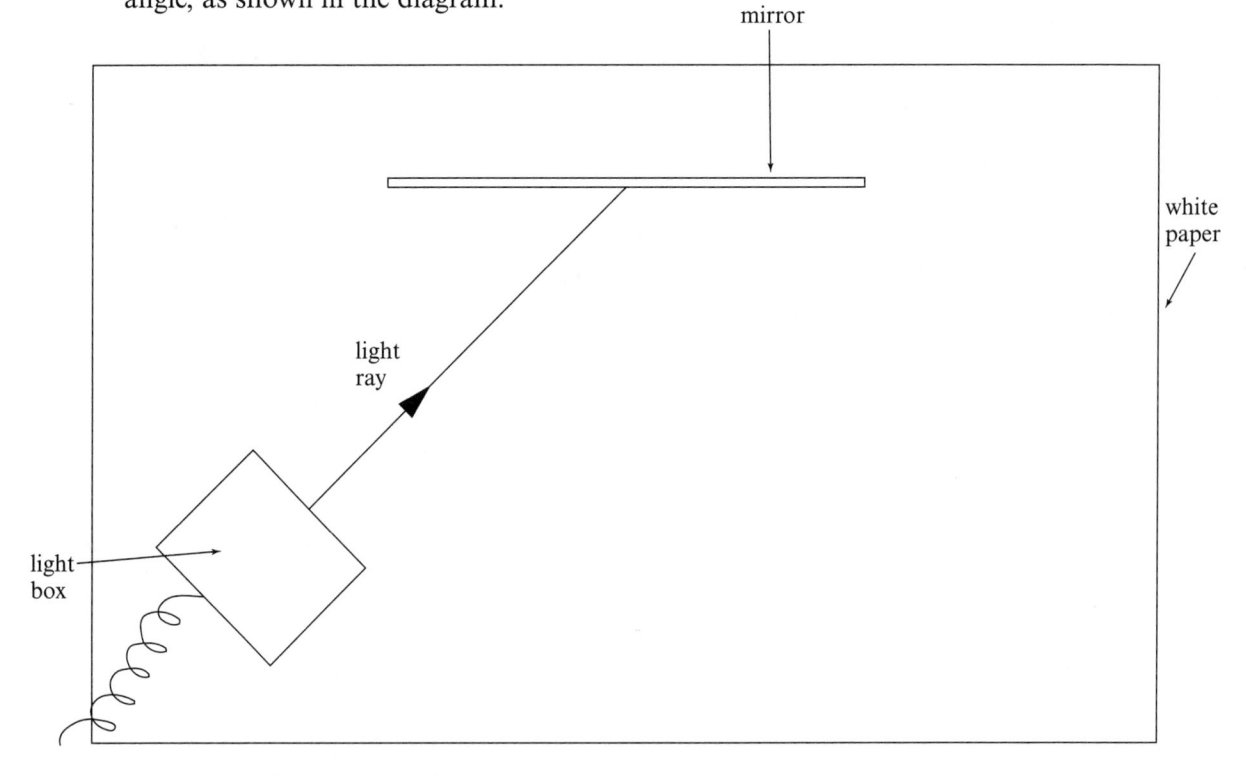

(i) Draw a **normal** on the diagram at the point where the light meets the mirror. **(1 mark)**

(ii) Draw a line on the diagram to show where the reflected light will go. (Use a ruler.) **(1 mark)**

(iii) State the law that you used to work out where the reflected light would go.

....

(1 mark)

(b) The student then points the beam of light at a rectangular block of glass. She notices that the light changes direction as it goes in and out of the block.

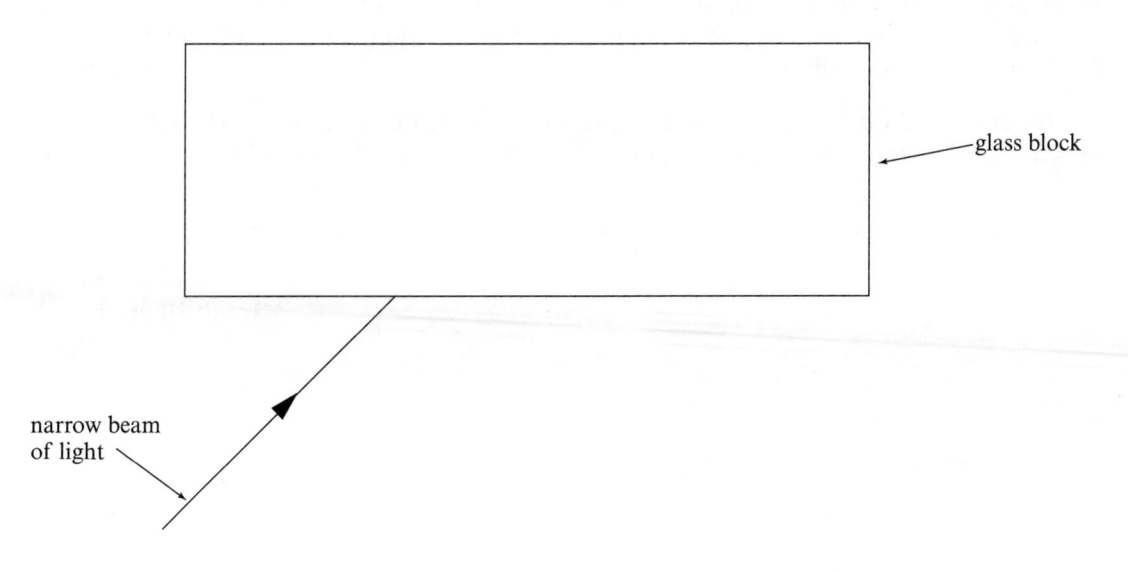

Turn over

(i) Draw on the diagram the path that you expect the light to take. (Use a ruler.) **(2 marks)**

(ii) What is the name for this change of direction when a wave goes from one material to another?

.... **(1 mark)**

(iii) What change to the wave makes it go in a different direction?

....

(1 mark)

(c) The rectangular block is exchanged for a semi-circular one.
A narrow light beam is then sent in, as shown on the diagram.

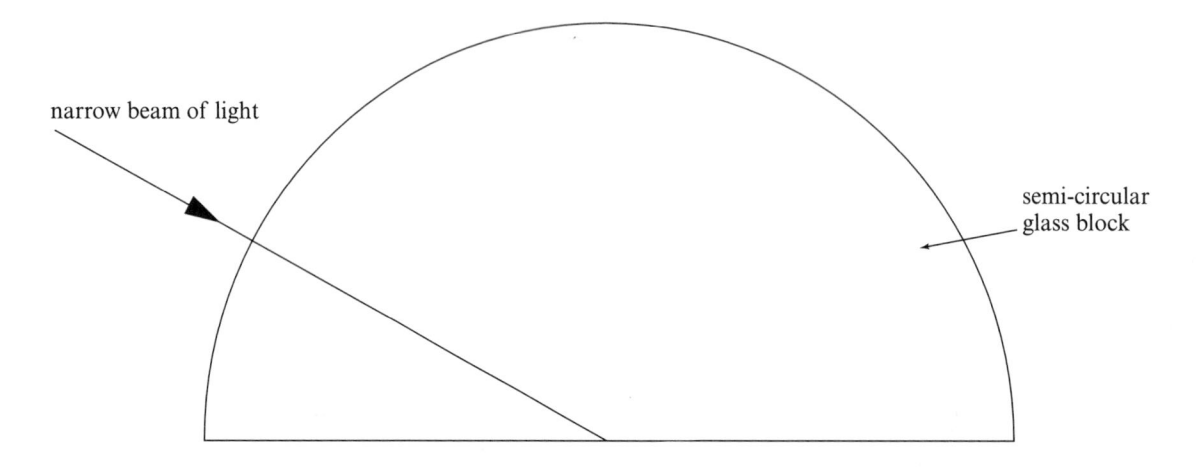

(i) Draw a line on the diagram to show where the light will go. (Use a ruler.) **(1 mark)**

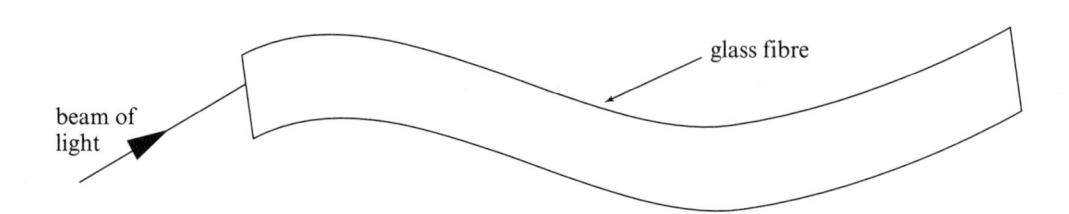

(ii) The diagram shows a beam of light going into one end of a thin glass fibre. Use the effect that is shown by the semi-circular block to complete the path of the ray of light along the glass fibre. **(1 mark)**

(iii) Bundles of optical fibres are made which can carry light in this way even when the fibres are bent so that they will go round corners. Name a use for these fibres.

....

(1 mark)
Total: 10 marks

9. (a) The captain of a ship that is a long way out at sea wishes to talk to his base.

   (i) Explain why he uses a satellite as shown in the diagram.

   ....

   ....

   (1 mark)

   (ii) What sort of waves will he use to send his signal to the satellite?

   ....

   (1 mark)

   (iii) He finds that the satellite is always above the same place on the earth whenever he wishes to use it. Explain what the orbit of the satellite is like for this to happen.

   ....

   ....

   (2 marks)

(b) The satellite has large panels on each side of it.
   (i) Explain what these panels are used for.

   ....

   ....

   (1 mark)

   (ii) Why don't the large panels slow the satellite down?

   ....

   (1 mark)

   (iii) The main part of the satellite would quickly overheat if it was not protected from radiation. Suggest a suitable method of doing this.

   ....

   (1 mark)

Turn over

*** (c) (i) Some other satellites are in a **polar orbit**.
Explain what is meant by a polar orbit.

....

....
(1 mark)

(ii) Explain why a satellite in a polar orbit has different uses from a geostationary satellite. Name one use.

....

.... **(1 mark)**

Use .... **(1 mark)**

(iii) In either type of orbit the satellite is moving at high speed.
Briefly explain why the satellite does not go off into space, and why it stays in orbit.

....

....
(2 marks)
Foundation Tier – Total: 7 marks
Higher Tier – Total: 12 marks

10. (a) Jaqui has made a cold drink by putting an ice cube into a glass of fizzy lemonade.

She realises that the glass now contains a **solid**, a **liquid** and a **gas**.
Her younger brother asks her what the difference is between these three states.

To help her explanation she uses three diagrams.

Each diagram shows how the particles are arranged in one of the states.

(i) Complete the other two diagrams using the same circle symbols to show particles.
(2 marks)

(ii) Which of the states will contain the fastest moving particles? .... **(1 mark)**

(iii) Which of the states will contain particles in a crystal structure? .... **(1 mark)**

(iv) Which of the states will have the lowest density? .... **(1 mark)**

(v) Jaqui's brother is watching the bubbles form and he thinks that they are appearing from nothing on the bottom of the glass.

What should Jaqui tell him to explain what is really happening to the gas particles?

....

....

(2 marks)

(b) The changes between the three states are shown in the diagram.

solid ⇌ liquid (A forward, B reverse)
E, C, F, D arrows to gas

Which of the changes A, B, C, D, E, F represents

(i) An ice cube melting .... **(1 mark)**

(ii) The water boiling in a kettle .... **(1 mark)**

(iii) Water vapour condensing on a cold window .... **(1 mark)**

(c) A mountaineer uses a stove that is fuelled by a small cylinder of propane.

(i) Propane is a gas which turns into a liquid under pressure.
Why is this preferred to using another gas which does not become a liquid at room temperature?

....

(1 mark)

(ii) He notices that when he uses the stove the fuel cylinder gets very cold and ice forms on its outside.
Explain why the cylinder becomes so cold.

....

....

....

(2 marks)

***(iii) When the mountaineer uses the stove he finds that it takes 15 minutes to raise the temperature of 500 g of water from 5 °C to 75 °C.
If it takes 4200 J of energy to change the temperature of 1 kg by each 1 °C, how much energy does the stove put into the water?

....

....

....

Energy = ... joules   **(2 marks)**

Turn over

What is the power of the stove as it heats the water?

....

....

Energy = ... watts

(2 marks)
Foundation Tier – Total: 13 marks
Higher Tier – Total: 17 marks

Longman
Examination Board

General Certificate of Secondary Education
Physics
Paper 2

Foundation

Time: 1 hour 15 minutes

Instructions

- For the Foundation Tier paper you should do all of the questions *except* those marked ***.
- Answer the questions in the spaces provided.

Higher

Time: 1 hour 30 minutes

Instructions

- For the Higher Tier paper you should do all of the questions *including* those marked ***.
- Answer the questions in the spaces provided.

Name ....

There is a list of formulae that you may use on page 2.

Number	Mark
1.	
2.	
3.	
4.	
5.	
6.	
7.	
8.	
9.	
10.	

---

1. (a) Adam has bought a compass. The compass contains a needle that has one half painted red. The needle is balanced at its centre so that it can turn freely.

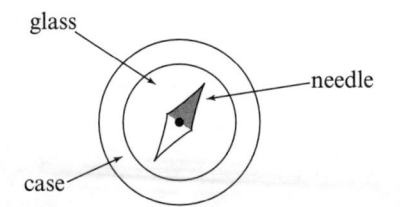

    When he puts the compass on a table, he finds that the red end of the needle points north.

    Adam brings one end of a small bar magnet next to the compass and it repels the red end of the compass needle.

Leave margin blank

21 **Turn over**

(i) Which pole is the end of the bar magnet that Adam tested? .... **(1 mark)**

(ii) What will happen if Adam brings the other end of the bar magnet near to the red end of the compass needle?

....

(1 mark)

(iii) Which metal is most likely to be contained in the needle?

.... **(1 mark)**

(iv) A recycling company is collecting aluminium cans from Adam's school but they do not want any steel cans.
Explain how Adam can use his compass to check that the cans are all aluminium.

....

....

(1 mark)

(b) Adam finds that the bar magnet makes a force on magnetic materials in the space around it. This is called its **magnetic field**.
To find out about this field he puts it on to a piece of plain paper and sprinkles iron filings around it.
On the diagram, draw the pattern that he will produce.

[Diagram: plain paper with bar magnet labelled S magnet N]

(2 marks)

(c) Michael has been told that a magnet can also be made by winding a coil of wire round a nail and connecting the wire to a battery.

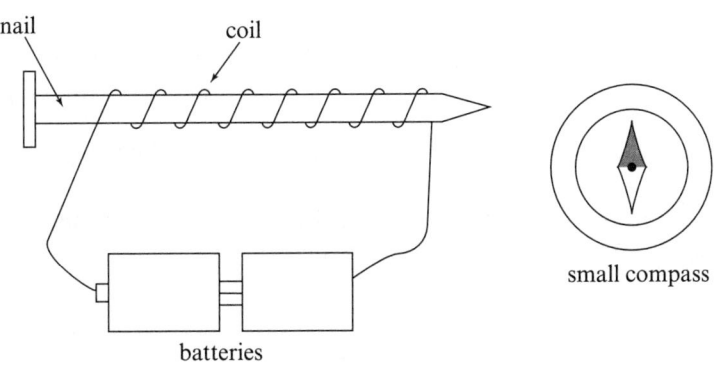

He makes the electromagnet and brings it close to Adam's compass as shown in the diagram.

(i) How will Michael know when his electromagnet is working?

....

(1 mark)

(ii) Michael tests the strength of his magnet by using it to pick up paper clips. Suggest **two** ways in which the electromagnet can be made stronger.

1. ....

2. .... **(2 marks)**

(iii) Michael makes a second electromagnet by winding the wire round a pencil instead of a nail. What effect does this have on the strength of the magnet?

....

(1 mark)

(d) A large electromagnet can be used to pick up metal scrap.
This sort of electromagnet will be much larger and will be powered by the 'mains' electricity supply which is a.c.

(i) What will the operator do to drop the scrap?

....

(1 mark)

(ii) What effect will the a.c. have on the poles of the magnet?

....

(1 mark)

(iii) What other advantage does the electromagnet have when used in this way?

....

(1 mark)
Total: 13 marks

Turn over

2. Amit can see a thunderstorm from the front window of his house.
   (a) Why does he hear the thunder **after** he sees the lightning?

   ....

   (1 mark)

   (b) He has a stopwatch and measures the time between seeing a flash and hearing the thunder. It is 3 seconds.
   He looks up the speed of sound in his Science book and finds that it is 340 m/s.
   Calculate how far the lightning flash was from Amit's house.

   ....

   ....

   ....

   (2 marks)

   (c) Some sound has a **frequency** which is above our hearing range.

   (i) What is this sort of sound called? .... **(1 mark)**

   (ii) Name a use for this sort of sound. .... **(1 mark)**

   (iii) What is meant by frequency? .... **(1 mark)**

   (iv) What are the units that we use when we measure frequency? .... **(1 mark)**

   Total: 7 marks

3. Marie is investigating the metal from which a ball bearing is made.
   (a) Explain how she can find the volume of the metal.

   ....

   ....

   ....

   ....

   (3 marks)

   (b) When Marie carries out her experiment she finds that the volume is 1.4 cm^3.
   She then puts the ball bearing on a balance and finds that its mass is 11.2 g.
   Use Marie's answers to work out the density of the metal.

   ....

   ....

   ....

   (2 marks)

(c) If Marie accidentally drops her ball bearing, it quickly falls to the ground. When she drops some paper of about the same weight it takes longer to reach the ground. Explain why this happens.

....

....

(1 mark)
Total: 6 marks

4. (a) Use words from the following list to fill in the spaces in the following sentences.

light years   solar system   the Milky Way   towards us   blue   galaxy

gravity   red   away from us   centrifugal   miles

Very large numbers of stars form a group called a............................ Our nearest star is the

Sun which belongs to a galaxy called .... The galaxies are very

big distances apart and we measure the distance in ....

We believe that the galaxies are moving ....

We know this because the light from distant galaxies is shifted towards the ....

The Sun is at the centre of the .... and attracts all the planets

with a force caused by .... so that they are all kept in their orbits.   **(7 marks)**

(b) Use the following table of information to answer the questions below.

Planet	Diameter/km	Orbital period/h	Gravity/N/kg	Rotation period/h
Mercury	4880	2100	4	1400
Venus	12 100	5400	9	5800
Earth	12 750	8760	10	24
	6800	16 500	4	24
Jupiter	142 800	104 000	26	10
Saturn	120 000	258 200	12	10
Uranus	52 800	736 400	9	17
Neptune	48 400	1 444 500	12	20
Pluto	3000	2 171 200	1	150

(i) The name of the fourth planet has been left out of the table.

Its name is ....   **(1 mark)**

(ii) Which planet is the smallest? ....   **(1 mark)**

(iii) How long is a year on Saturn? ....   **(1 mark)**

(iv) How long is a day on Venus? ....   **(1 mark)**

Turn over

(v) If a space probe of mass 150 kg reached Jupiter what would it weigh? .... **(1 mark)**

(vi) Mercury has a much higher surface temperature than Earth.
Explain why this happens.

....

....

(1 mark)

***(vii) The surface temperature of Venus is actually higher than that of Mercury.
We believe that Venus has an atmosphere that contains a lot of dense gases such as carbon dioxide.
Explain how the atmosphere of the planet might change its expected temperature.

....

....

(2 marks)

(c) A comet is not a planet or a moon but it does orbit the Sun.
  (i) State one difference between a comet and a planet or moon.

....

(1 mark)

(ii) The diagram below shows the orbit of a comet round the Sun.

What force keeps the comet in its orbit round the Sun? .... **(1 mark)**

Why is the force larger at B than at A? .... **(1 mark)**

Foundation Tier – Total: 16 marks
Higher Tier – Total: 18 marks

5. Joanne uses a converging (convex) lens to form the image of a candle on a screen.

   (a) Draw the image of the candle on the screen. **(2 marks)**

   (b) Joanne then moves the candle further from the lens.
       (i) Which way will she need to move the screen to get a clear sharp image again?

       ....
       (1 mark)

       (ii) What will happen to the size of the image when she does this?

       ....
       (1 mark)

   (c) Joanne knows that it is sometimes important to know the focal length of a lens. Explain how she could measure the approximate focal length of the convex lens.

   ....

   ....

   ....
   (2 marks)

   (d) The diagram shows a concave (diverging) lens.

       (i) Complete the path of the rays through the lens. **(2 marks)**

       (ii) Name one use for this type of lens. .... **(1 mark)**

       Total: 9 marks

       Turn over

6. (a) Fill in the missing words in the following description of how electricity can be produced.

If a wire is moved so that it cuts through a magnetic .... then a voltage

will be .... in the wire. This effect is called electromagnetic ....

(3 marks)

(b) The effect described in part (a) can be shown by doing the following experiment:

When the magnet is put into the coil, the meter shows a small reading.

(i) What sort of meter will be needed for the experiment? .... **(1 mark)**

(ii) What will the meter show when the magnet stops inside the coil?

....

(1 mark)

(iii) The magnet is now removed very quickly from the coil.
What will be seen on the meter?

....

(2 marks)

(iv) Another coil is made with more turns of wire.
What difference will this make to the readings on the meter when the experiment is done again?

....

(1 mark)

(c) Many modern appliances contain electronic parts. If they are to be used on the 'mains' electricity supply the voltage has to be changed.
(i) Why does the voltage have to be changed?

....

(1 mark)

(ii) One way to change voltages is to use a transformer.

In this case the primary coil of the transformer has 180 turns and the secondary coil has 4600 turns. If the primary coil is connected to 230 V, what will the output from the secondary coil be?

....

....

....

(2 marks)

(iii) Which metal will the core be made from? .... **(1 mark)**

(iv) Why will a transformer NOT work with a d.c. supply?

....

(1 mark)

***(d) If a d.c. output is needed, some additional components will be added.

Name the extra components, A and B, and state briefly what each one does.

Name of A .... **(1 mark)**

Function of A .... **(1 mark)**

Name of B .... **(1 mark)**

Function of B .... **(1 mark)**

Foundation Tier – Total: 13 marks
Higher Tier – Total: 17 marks

Turn over

7. (a) Angela went to a caravan site in Italy for her holidays.
She noticed that there was a large solar panel on the roof of the shower block.

   (i) The surface of the solar panel was painted black. Why was this colour chosen?

   ....

   (1 mark)

   (ii) A water pipe went from the shower block into the bottom of the panel and another pipe left the panel at the top to take the water back to the shower block.
   Why were these pipes covered in plastic foam?

   ....

   (1 mark)

   Which of the two pipes will carry the hottest water? .... **(1 mark)**

   (iii) The pipe inside the plastic foam could be made from plastic, copper, iron or glass.
   Which material do you think was chosen, and for what reason?

   Material .... **(1 mark)**

   Reason .... **(1 mark)**

   (iv) Angela noticed that the water was not as hot when she used the showers in the morning as it had been in the evening. Why was this?

   ....

   (1 mark)

   (v) During the afternoon on a very hot day the white wall of the caravan was quite warm. The roof of her dark blue car parked next to the caravan was very hot.
   Explain why the two surfaces were at different temperatures.

   ....

   (1 mark)

   (vi) The caravan is fitted with window blinds that are silvered on their outside surface.
   Explain how these can be used to keep the caravan at a more pleasant temperature.

   ....

   .... **(1 mark)**

(b) Most of the food in the caravan could be kept cool in the refrigerator, but some was taken out during the day for picnics. This food was carried in a 'cool-box'.

(i) The diagram shows the construction of the sides of the cool-box. Why are the walls of the box made in this particular way?

....

....

(2 marks)

(ii) The box has a lid made from the same material as the sides and bottom. The lid is a tight fit into the box. Why is this important?

....

(1 mark)

(iii) Which part of the box will be at the lowest temperature? (Explain your answer.)

....

....

(2 marks)

(c) The caravan has a cable that connects with the 'mains' electricity on the site so that the fridge and lights all work. The supply from the site has a circuit breaker that switches off if the current reaches 3 A.

(i) Angela wishes to use her electric hair drier. The information on the drier says 230V a.c. 1200 W. Can she use this drier in the caravan? (Show your working clearly.)

....

....

....

(3 marks)

*** (ii) The caravan is not properly earthed as a house would be. What other device must the caravan have and what will it do?

....

....

(2 marks)

(d) When the caravan is loaded and connected to the car, it pushes down on the back of the car with a force of 750 N as shown in the diagram below.

The distance from this force to the axle is 5 m.

Turn over

(i) Calculate the turning moment of the force about the axle.

....

.... **(2 marks)**

Turning moment = ... Nm.

(ii) If this force becomes much greater than 750 N the caravan may become dangerous when it is towed. What could you do to make the force less?

....

(1 mark)

(e) When the caravan is being towed, the acceleration is a lot less than when the car is being driven on its own. Explain why this happens.

....

....

(1 mark)
Foundation Tier – Total: 20 marks
Higher Tier – Total: 22 marks

8. (a) The circuit shown below contains an LDR.

   (i) What do the letters LDR stand for?

   ....

   ....

   (1 mark)

   (ii) Describe and explain what will happen if the light shining on the LDR becomes brighter.

   ....

   ....

   (2 marks)

(b) In the second circuit, shown below, the LDR and a resistor have been connected across a 9 V battery. A voltmeter is connected across the resistor.

   (i) Describe and explain what happens to the reading on the voltmeter as the light on the LDR is increased.

   ....

   ....

   ....

   ....

   (2 marks)

(ii) The resistor that is used has a resistance of 1000 Ω.
If the current through the resistor is 5 mA (0.005 A), what is the p.d. across the resistor?

....

....

....

(3 marks)

(c) The LDR and resistor are used as one of the sensors in the following circuit.

The circuit is put into an animal house at a zoo so that the heater comes on if it is too cold at night.

(i) Three of the components are the logic gates X, Y and Z.
Name these logic gates.

X .... Y .... Z .... **(3 marks)**

(ii) Explain briefly what component X does in this circuit.

....

....

(2 marks)

(iii) When would the heater be switched on if X was left out of this circuit?

....

(1 mark)

(iv) What device will be used by the temperature sensor to detect changes in temperature?

.... **(1 mark)**

(v) Complete the following truth table for the circuit shown. The table shows the state of the heater and the state of each of the sensors.

Light sensor	Temperature sensor	Heater
0		1
	1	
1	1	0

(3 marks)

Turn over

***(vi) The truth table shows that the three gates X, Y, Z could be replaced by a single gate. What is the name of this gate?

.... **(1 mark)**

***(vii) The circuit includes a relay. Explain why this is needed.

....

(1 mark)

***(d) In the real circuit for the animal house, the relay coil has another component connected across it as shown in the following diagram.

(i) What is the name of this component?

.... **(1 mark)**

(ii) What does this component do?

....

.... **(1 mark)**

Foundation Tier – Total: 18 marks
Higher Tier – Total: 22 marks

*** 9. A radio transmitter sends radio waves past the top of a cliff as shown on the diagram below.

A listener in the house at X receives the waves, but the signal is not very strong.

(i) Draw more waves on the diagram to show how the waves reach the house. **(1 mark)**

(ii) What is the name for this effect? .... **(1 mark)**

(iii) The radio transmitter is also sending out a different signal using longer waves. The listener in the house tunes his receiver to this signal. Explain the difference that the listener notices compared with the first signal.

....

....

(2 marks)
Higher Tier – Total 4 marks

10.

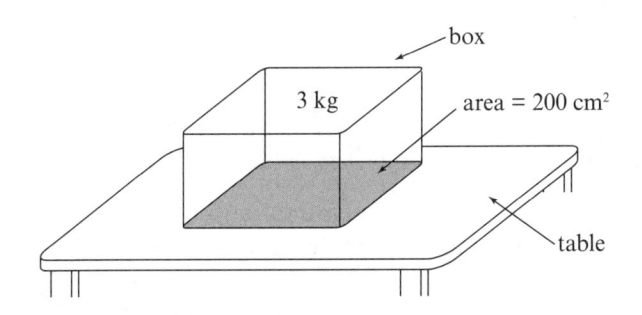

(a) (i) This box is resting on a table and it has a mass of 3 kg.
The strength of gravity (g) is 10 N/kg. What is the weight of the box?

....

....
(1 mark)

(ii) Write down the formula that connects pressure with force and area.

....

....
(1 mark)

(iii) The area that the box is resting on is 200 cm².
What is the pressure on the table caused by the box?

....

....
(2 marks)

(b) John notices that pressing his thumb on a noticeboard does not make a mark. When he presses the point of a drawing pin on the board with the same force it goes easily into the board. Explain why this happens.

....

....
(2 marks)

(c) A small car has been designed to work as a robot on Mars.
The car has wide, soft tyres instead of narrow, hard ones. Explain why you think this will be an advantage.

....

(2 marks)

Turn over

(d) A cylinder of gas has a volume of 5 litres.
The gas inside it is at a pressure of 20 atmospheres.
 (i) What would the volume of the gas become at 1 atmosphere if it stayed at the same temperature?

 ....

 ....
 (2 marks)

 (ii) The tap on the cylinder was left open so that the gas slowly leaked into the air. What was the pressure of the gas when it stopped leaking from the cylinder?

 ....
 (1 mark)

 (iii) What volume of gas will be left in the cylinder when it stops leaking?

 ....
 (1 mark)

 (iv) How much gas will have escaped into the air from the cylinder?

 ....
 (1 mark)

***(e) A cylinder of gas is taken out into space for use on a space station.
When it is in space the gas does not have a weight.
The gas still has a pressure, but the pressure cannot be caused by the weight of the gas.
Explain what does cause the pressure of the gas.

....

....
(2 marks)

***(f) An aerosol can is often used for spray paints. The gas inside is at a greater pressure than the air outside, so that the paint is pushed out when the valve is opened.

Use your ideas about gas pressure to explain why it would be dangerous to throw a used aerosol can on to a fire.

....

....
(2 marks)
Foundation Tier – Total: 13 marks
Higher Tier – Total: 17 marks

Longman Examination Board

General Certificate of Secondary Education
Physics
Paper 3

This paper is shorter than the other two and is intended for you to use closer to the final examinations, when you may have less time available.

Foundation

Time: 1 hour

Instructions

- For the Foundation Tier paper you should do all of the questions *except* those marked ***.
- Section A is multiple choice. For each question, circle the letter corresponding to the correct answer.
- For section B answer the questions in the spaces provided.

Higher

Time: 1 hour 15 minutes

Instructions

- For the Higher Tier paper you should do all of the questions *including* those marked ***.
- Section A is multiple choice. For each question, circle the letter corresponding to the correct answer.
- For section B answer the questions in the spaces provided.

Name ....

There is a list of formulae that you may use on page 2.

Number	Mark
Section A 1–20.	
Section B 21.	
22.	
23.	
24.	
25.	
26.	

Turn over

Section A   Allow 25 minutes for this section

Each of these questions has one mark for a correct answer.

1. A polythene rod has a negative charge after being rubbed with a piece of cloth. This is because:

   A. Positive charges have been taken off the rod and put on to the cloth

   B. Electrons are rubbed off the cloth by friction and put on to the rod

   C. Electrons are rubbed off the rod by friction and put on to the cloth

   D. Positive charges have been rubbed off the cloth and put on to the rod

   E. Heat produced by friction has turned into electrical energy

2. Which of the following appliances would not be connected to a ring main in the home?

   A. a television   B. an electric cooker   C. a radio   D. a hair drier   E. a food mixer

3. Potential difference is measured in

   A. volts   B. amps   C. ohms   D. watts   E. joules

4. A magnet is pushed into a coil of wire which has a voltmeter connected across its ends. Which of the following statements is NOT true?

   A. Moving the magnet faster produces a bigger voltage.

   B. Reversing the direction of movement of the magnet reverses the direction of the voltage produced.

   C. Moving the coil towards the magnet has the same effect as moving the magnet towards the coil.

   D. Adding more turns to the coil increases the voltage produced.

   E. Using a stronger magnet still produces the same voltage.

5. A circuit designer needs a component to store some electric charge. The stored charge can then be used to smooth out changes in the current in the circuit.
   The component that he uses could be:

   A. a diode   B. a capacitor   C. a transistor   D. a resistor   E. an LDR

6. A racing cyclist covers 1200 m in one minute. His average speed is:

   A. 18 m/s   B. 12 m/s   C. 20 m/s   D. 2 m/s   E. 200 m/s

7. A spring is 10 cm long. When a force of 1 N is applied to it, the spring becomes 12 cm long. What is the total length of the spring when a force of 3 N is applied?

   A. 16 cm   B. 13 cm   C. 36 cm   D. 30 cm   E. 15 cm

8. The diagram shows a uniform metre rule pivoted at its centre. The metre rule is balanced.

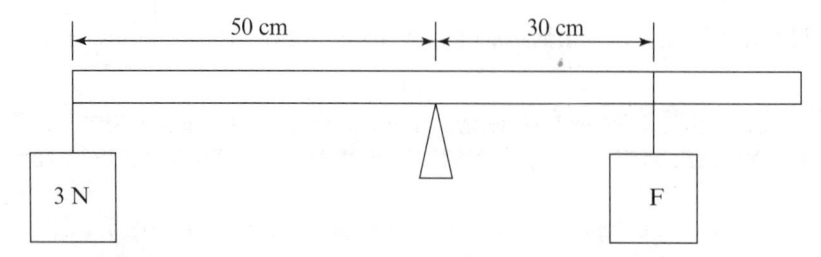

   What is the force F?

   A. 1.8 N   B. 2.0 N   C. 3.0 N   D. 5.0 N   E. 8.0 N

9. Which of the following waves is not transverse?

   A. light   B. sound   C. X-rays   D. ultra-violet   E. gamma rays

10. We can see both the sun and the moon from earth. Which line in the table below explains why?

	The sun	The moon
A.	gives out light	gives out light
B.	reflects light	gives out light
C.	reflects light	reflects light
D.	gives out light	is very close to Earth
E.	gives out light	reflects light

11. John records what the moon looks like each night. How long will it be before he can see the moon looking the same as it did on the first night?

    A. 24 hours   B. one week   C. 28 days   D. one year   E. it never looks exactly the same again

12. The diagram shows white light shining on to a red filter.

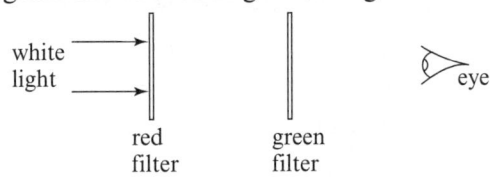

    What will a person on the other side of the green filter see?

    A. yellow light   B. red light   C. blue light   D. no light (black)   E. magenta light

13. Which of the following describes what the iris does in the eye?

    A. It changes the size of the image on the retina.
    B. It controls the amount of light that enters the eye.
    C. It helps to focus the light on to the retina.
    D. It controls the size of the lens in the eye.
    E. It receives the image and sends it on to the brain through the optic nerve.

14. Which of the following statements is **true** according to kinetic theory?

    A. The particles in liquids have spaces between them so that the liquid can flow.
    B. The particles in a gas are more widely spaced than those in solids and liquids.
    C. All the particles in a liquid have their own place in the liquid structure.
    D. The particles in a liquid can only vibrate but do so faster as the temperature rises.
    E. The particles in a gas do not change their speed much when the temperature increases.

15. An electric heater is put into a polystyrene beaker containing some liquid. The temperature of the liquid is then raised from room temperature to its boiling point.
    Which of the following statements is true?

    A. The time taken to do this depends only on the power of the heater.
    B. The amount of thermal energy needed to raise the temperature will depend on the specific heat capacity of the liquid.
    C. The amount of thermal energy needed will be the same no matter what mass of liquid is used because the temperature rise is always the same.
    D. The amount of thermal energy needed does not depend on the temperature rise.
    E. The temperature will continue to rise until all of the liquid has boiled away.

Turn over

16. Which of the lines in the table shows the correct units for the quantities named at the top of each column?

	Energy	Weight
A.	newtons	kilograms
B.	joules	kilograms
C.	watts	newtons
D.	joules	newtons
E.	watts	watts

17. Which of the following statements is correct?

   A. All machines have an efficiency better than 100%.

   B. Efficiency can be measured by the amount of energy lost.

   C. Efficiency = $\dfrac{\text{energy output}}{\text{energy input}}$

   D. Low efficiency is caused by energy being destroyed in the machine.

   E. Efficiency is measured in watts.

18. There are several types of radioactivity, each of which has different properties.
    Which one of the following is a correct description of the beta radiation given out by some radioactive materials?

   A. Particles that carry a positive charge and are the same as the nucleus of a helium atom.

   B. Particles that are high speed electrons with a negative charge.

   C. Waves that are only stopped by a few centimetres of lead.

   D. Waves that carry large amounts of energy but no mass or charge.

   E. Positively charged particles that are detected best by a photographic plate.

19. Which row of the following table correctly shows the mass and charge for the particle named?

	Particle	Mass	Charge
A.	electron	−1	0
B.	proton	1	0
C.	neutron	1	−1
D.	proton	1	1
E.	neutron	1	1

20. Terminal velocity is the constant speed that is eventually reached by a falling object in a gas or a liquid. Which of the following statements is true?

   A. At terminal velocity there are no forces acting.

   B. At terminal velocity the weight is equal and opposite to the drag.

   C. Terminal velocity on the moon is less than on the earth.

   D. At terminal velocity the weight is still greater than the drag.

   E. At terminal velocity the upward force of the drag is bigger than the weight.

Total: 20 marks

Paper 3 – Foundation and Higher 41

Section B Allow 35 minutes for this section if you are doing the Foundation Tier.
Allow 50 minutes if you are doing the Higher Tier.

***21. A sample of radioactive material was collected in a school laboratory and its activity recorded using a Geiger counter.
After correcting for background count the results were as follows.

Time (sec)	0	30	60	90	120	150	180	210	240	270
Counts per sec	1000	725	535	415	320	225	175	75	95	70

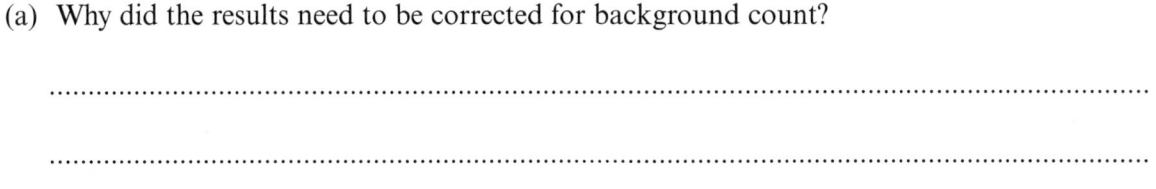

(a) Why did the results need to be corrected for background count?

....

....
(1 mark)

(b) Plot a graph of the data in the table. **(3 marks)**

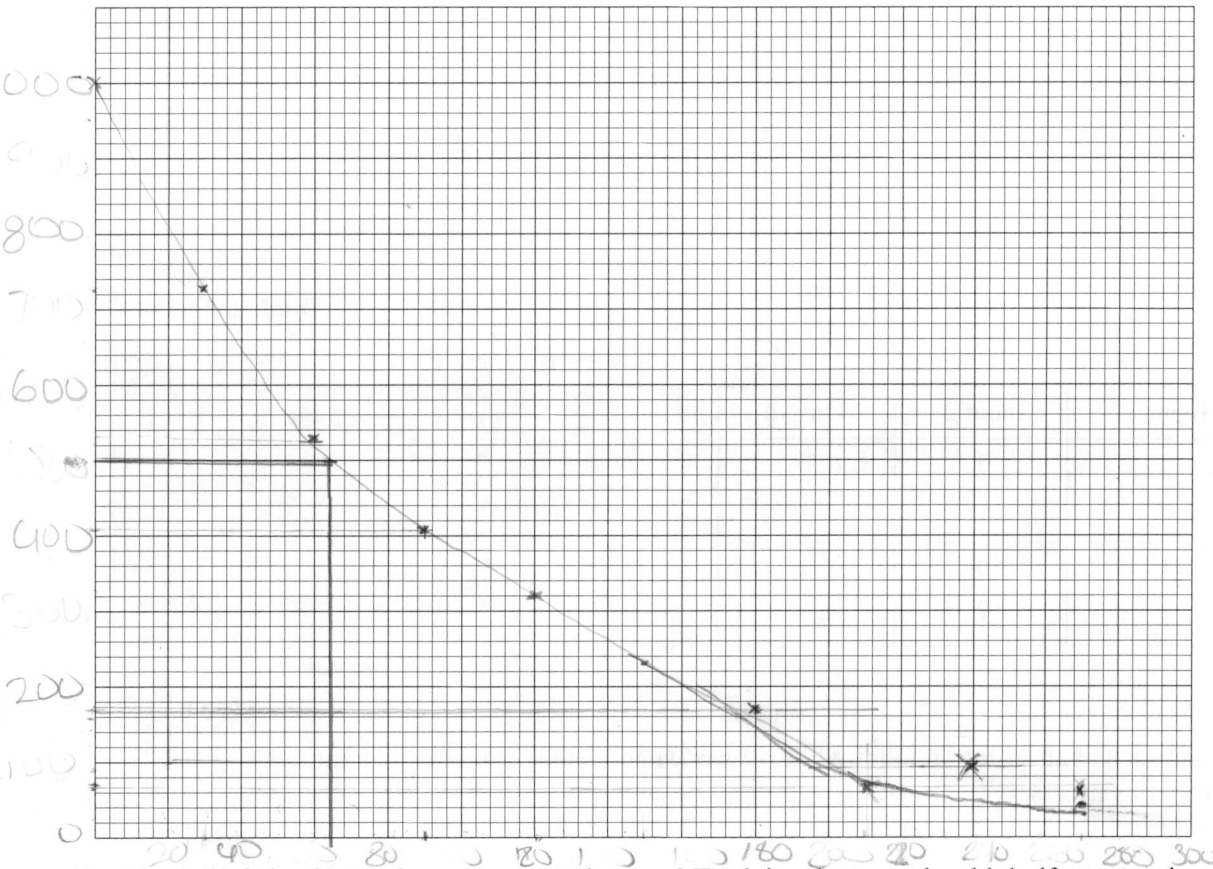

(c) Were all of the data points on a smooth curve? Explain what you should do if some points are found to be close to, but not on, the same curve as the others.

....

....
(2 marks)

Turn over

(d) Use the graph to determine the half-life of the substance.
Show any working clearly.

64 sec

The half-life is .... **(3 marks)**

(e) Explain why this material was suitable for a class experiment.

because it took a short amount of time to decay

(1 mark)
Higher Tier – Total: 10 marks

22. There are a number of uses for radioactive materials.
(a) Name or **briefly** describe a medical use for radioactivity.

gamma rays are used to treat cancers.

(1 mark)

(b) Name or **briefly** describe an industrial use for radioactive materials.

buildings leak detections γ or β

(1 mark)
Total: 2 marks

23. (a) What is the name of the logic gate that has the following truth table?

Input 1	Input 2	Output
0	0	0
0	1	1
1	0	1
1	1	1

The gate is .... **(1 mark)**

(b) A gate such as this is often followed by a relay when it is used in a real circuit. Why is this necessary?

....

(1 mark)
Total: 2 marks

24. A ray of light inside a glass fibre is totally internally reflected when it meets the air at the surface of the glass at an angle greater than the **critical angle**.

(a) What happens if the angle is less than the critical angle?

....

(1 mark)

(b) What is meant by 'totally internally reflected'?

....

....

(1 mark)

(c) Complete the paths of the rays of light through the two glass prisms in the diagram.

(2 marks)

(d) (i) Name an optical instrument that uses total internal reflection in prisms.

....

(1 mark)

(ii) What is the advantage of using prisms in the application that you named?

....

(1 mark)
Total: 6 marks

25. (a) (i) Heat loss through the ceilings and the roof of a house is quite a large fraction of the total. State how this can be reduced.

....

(1 mark)

(ii) Explain how the method you have chosen would reduce the heat loss.

....

....

(1 mark)

(b) Name one other place where heat is lost from a house and describe briefly how you would reduce it.

....

....

....

(2 marks)
Total: 4 marks

Turn over

26. (a) A pupil wires up the circuit shown in the diagram below.

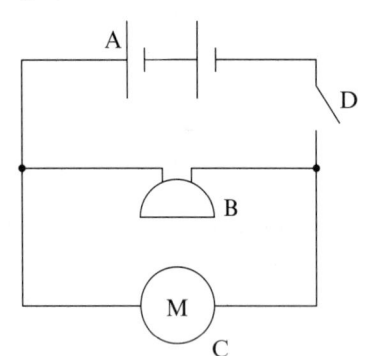

(i) Name the parts of the circuit shown by the symbols labelled A, B, C and D:

A .... B ....

C .... D .... **(4 marks)**

(ii) When the circuit is switched on, an energy transfer takes place. Complete the energy transfer diagram to show what is happening in this circuit.

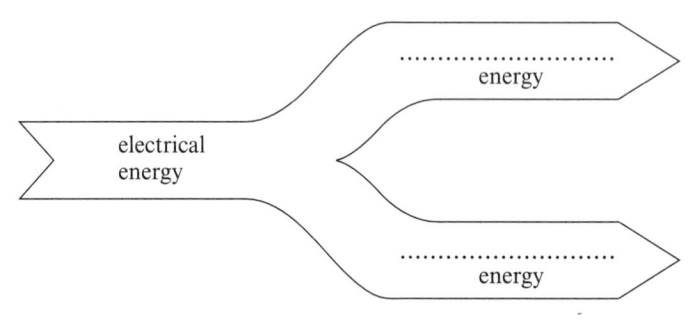

(2 marks)

(iii) When the circuit is working a current of 2 A passes through the battery. The current is left on for 3 minutes. How much charge has been transferred round the circuit in this time?

....

....

....

(3 marks)

(iv) When the battery supplies 2 A of current, component C has a current of 1.75 A. How much current is being supplied to component B?

.... **(1 mark)**

(b) The same components are rewired so that they are connected in series using the same battery as before. The new circuit is shown in the diagram below.

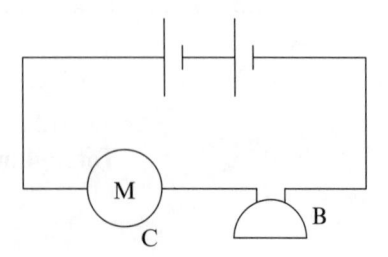

(i) Will the current now be greater than, less than or still equal to 2 A?

.... **(1 mark)**

(ii) Explain what happens to component C in this new circuit if component B stops working.

....

(2 marks)

(c) A student connects a battery across a bulb. The bulb is marked 3 V 0.5 A.

(i) What is the resistance of the bulb?

....

....

....

(3 marks)

(ii) How much energy is converted by this bulb each minute?

....

....

....

(3 marks)
Total: 19 marks

Solutions to practice exam papers

Each * represents 1 mark. Make sure your answer is correct before you award yourself the mark – if you are not sure ask your teacher or another responsible person.

- The tips will help you with your revision.

- Always remember that there may be other correct answers that are not listed and might get credit. These are rare though and you should check VERY carefully before awarding yourself marks for anything not on the marking scheme. The most common problem is misreading a question and answering the question that you hope to find instead of the one that is really there – unfortunately you don't get credit for work that is not asked for even if its facts are correct!

- When there is more than one correct answer the ones that are acceptable will be separated by /. Any of the answers in the list will then be worth the mark.
Examiners often put 'wtte' on their mark schemes – this stands for 'words to that effect' and means that you don't need to have the exact words as long as it is clear what you mean.

Solutions to Paper 1

1. (a) (i) the arrow should be drawn in the tunnel pointing to the right*

    (ii) gravitational potential energy*

    (iii) kinetic energy (in the water) is transformed into electrical energy**
    (The marks are for naming the energy correctly. You can show the transformation as a flow diagram with an arrow between the two if you wish.)

    (iv) The water will still have some of the kinetic energy* when it shoots out of the tunnel and some energy is always turned into heat* by friction in bearings, etc. 1 mark for each of the 'other' two final forms of energy. **6 marks**

> **TIP**
> Energy is never created or destroyed but is transferred from one system to another where it may be in a different form. DON'T write an answer that suggests that some of the energy in the water disappears!

   (b) (i) A renewable energy resource is one that can be continually replaced and used again without the supply running out.**

    (ii) any two from: wind; wave; solar; tidal; biofuel**

    (iii) any two from: nuclear; coal; oil; natural gas** **6 marks**

   (c) (i) advantage – any one from: no pollutant waste created; no further fuel to buy after building; no pipeline/rail/road needed for fuel delivery*
    disadvantage – any one from: flooding of valley destroys crops/habitat; changes river flow downstream from dam*

    (ii) country with good oil or coal reserves would find them cheap to use*
    country without fossil fuels might opt for nuclear power as a reliable, non-weather-dependent source* **4 marks**
    (Remember that you need to name the resource AND give reasons for using it.)

   (d) Any two from: clean and doesn't create waste products; easy to 'transport'; can be used for a number of different applications (light/heat/motors, etc.)** **2 marks**

    Total: 18 marks

Solutions to Paper 1 ■ 47

2. (a) (i) bulb H*

   (ii) bulb H has three batteries connected across it, so it gets more p.d. than any other
   (I and J would be the next brightest, but each gets only half of the p.d. that is across H)*
   2 marks

(b) Circuit 1*   **1 mark**

> **TIP**
> All of the other circuits supply current to one bulb (like circuit 1) and then more current to another branch of the circuit in parallel with the bulb.

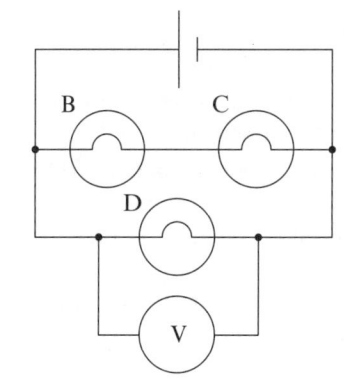

(c) voltmeter* connected across bulb D*   **2 marks**

(d)

Bulb	On or off
E	off*
F	on*
G	on*

3 marks
Total: 8 marks

3. (a) cable grip not used*; earth and neutral wires interchanged*   **2 marks**

> **TIP**
> Remember that interchanging the wires is only ONE mark because getting one of the wires wrong must mean that another is also wrong! Lots of students miss the cable grip – make sure that you also remember where each wire goes and that there should be no bare wires.

(b) the fuse protects the cable from overheating caused by the electric current being too big*
1 mark

> **TIP**
> The fuse is NOT there to prevent electric shock! The danger prevented is fire caused by an overheated cable.

(c) units = power × time = 0.9 × 5 = 4.5 kilowatt-hours*
cost = units × cost per unit = 4.5 × 8 = 36p*   **2 marks**

> **TIP**
> Even for a simple calculation like this, DO write down the working so that the examiner can still give you some credit if you make mistakes.

(d) (i) live and neutral**   **2 marks**

(ii) The appliance has been specially designed so that all live wires are carefully insulated. This means that even when there is a fault the wires cannot connect with the outside or with any metal parts.* **1 mark**

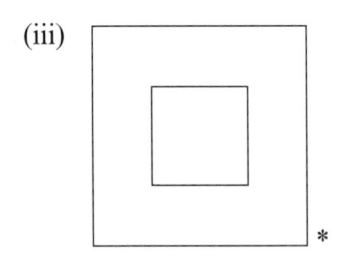

(iii)

*   **1 mark**

***(e)

> **TIP**
> This sort of answer is called a *free response*. It is used so you can show your ability to deal with a logical answer which needs a longer explanation rather than just short facts.
> You are looking for three marks here – one for what is meant by a ring main and the other two for the advantages.

(i) In a ring main, all the sockets on one floor of a house are connected in parallel on to one long cable. Both ends of the cable are connected to the consumer unit, so forming a ring round the house.* **1 mark**

(ii) Each socket is effectively connected to the consumer unit by two cables (i.e. both ways along the ring)* and a thinner (cheaper) cable can therefore be used to connect all the sockets than would be possible with one single cable.* **2 marks**

***(f) (i) a.c. stands for alternating current* **1 mark**

(ii) The current from batteries always flows the same way round a circuit; alternating current is driven first one way round the circuit and then the opposite way. (In 'mains' a.c. the current is reversed 100 times per second.)* **1 mark**

Total: 9 Foundation level marks + 5 additional Higher level marks

4. (a) In BC the train travels at a constant velocity of 30 m/s*; in CD the train slows to a stop (with uniform negative acceleration)* **2 marks**

(b)

> **TIP**
> You can use a formula or remember that the distance moved will be the same as the area under the graph. These methods are both correct and will both get full marks. Usually any CORRECT method will get full marks.

(i) distance = speed × time = 30 × 80 = 2400 m* **1 mark**

(ii) distance = area under graph = area rectangle + area triangle*
= (10 × 20) + (0.5 × 20 × 20) = 400 m*

or Distance = $\frac{(u + v)t^*}{2} = \frac{(10 + 30)20}{2}$ = 400 m* **2 marks**

(c) acceleration = $\frac{\text{change in velocity}}{\text{time taken}}$

= $\frac{20}{20}$ = 1 m/s² *answer *unit **2 marks**

(d) (i) force = mass × acceleration* **1 mark**

(ii) force = 20 000 × 1
     = 20 000 N** **2 marks**
(A very simple calculation. One of the marks is for the correct unit.
Check that you could also have found the braking force in CD (= −60 000 N).)

(e) Only one mark = one fact needed, so you can give yourself the mark for the energy becoming heat energy in the brakes.* The energy is then radiated into the air as infra-red waves or conducted into the train/ground/air. **1 mark**

***(f) KE = ½ × mass × velocity²*
      = ½ × 20 000 × 30²
      = 9 000 000 J (or 9 MJ)** answer* unit* **3 marks**

***(g) The springs will mean that it takes the train longer to stop*;
the longer time means that the acceleration is smaller*;
a smaller acceleration means a smaller force so that less damage is done* **3 marks**

Total: 11 Foundation level marks + 6 additional Higher level marks

> **TIP**
>
> This is a question with a number of calculations. This is common in Physics and you should remember to:
>
> ■ Show all your working, including the formulas you use.
>
> ■ Underline the final answer so that it is obvious and easy for the examiner to find.
>
> ■ Remember to include the correct unit unless it is given at the end of the answer space – not doing so often loses marks!

5. (a) (i) transmission of telephone calls/ communication with satellites/ ovens*

   (ii) sun beds/ forgery detection/ showing up marks from special pens for theft prevention*

   (iii) electric fires/ land inspection from satellites/ channel changers for TV*

   (iv) echo sounding/ internal body organ scans (pregnancies, kidneys, etc.)* **4 marks**

(b) (i) ultra-violet* (ii) ultrasound* (iii) ultrasound* (Don't be put off by having the same answer repeated.) **3 marks**

(c) (i) the pitch will be higher* (ii) the sound will be quieter* **2 marks**

(d) (i) speed = frequency × wavelength*
    (ii) speed = 5 × 25 = 125 cm/s* (Only one mark – no mark for the unit which is on the paper.) **2 marks**

(e) any two from: double glazing/ screens of trees or bushes/ sound insulation (foam, etc.) on the walls of the rooms. Cavity wall insulation and lots of soft furnishings might also help.** **2 marks**

(f) (i) permanent deafness (probably with some temporary deafness at the end of a day)*

   (ii) Wear ear defenders* (remember to try to use the correct words – in spite of their appearance ear defenders are not ear muffs or headphones!)

   (iii) decibels / dB* (take care with this unit – it is important to have a 'small' d and a 'capital' B.) **3 marks**

Total 16 marks

50 ■ Longman Practice Exam Papers

6. (a) (i) Background count*

    (ii) any two from: walls/ surrounding rock and stone/ building materials; cosmic radiation; food; discharge from the nuclear industry; fallout from nuclear weapon testing.** (There are two marks so expect to give at least two sources for the background radiation.) **3 marks**

   (b) (i) alpha*   (ii) symbol E*

    (iii) any two from: keep at a distance – handling tool; count all sources out AND back into the material safe; use sources that are as small as possible; avoid using sources that are powder or liquid.** **4 marks**

   (c) (i) it is an electromagnetic wave rather than a particle*

    (ii) one of: sterilising fruit/medical instruments; treating cancer; as a tracer*   **2 marks**

   (d) (i) beta*
     alpha will always be totally absorbed; gamma will not be absorbed much at all. Some beta will be absorbed, and the amount that penetrates through to the detector will depend on the foil thickness.*

    (ii) Surround the source with metal, such as thick aluminium, with the only hole to let out radiation pointing in the direction of the foil and detector.*   **3 marks**

   ***(iii) half-life is the time taken for half of the atoms of a radioactive isotope to decay.*
     It is important that the half-life is not so short that the readings will change over the lifetime of the machine.*   **2 marks**

*** (e) (i) 38*   (ii) 90*   **2 marks**

> **TIP**
> Remember that the easy way to do these is to add the numbers at the top on the left-hand side of the equation, which must equal the total at the top of the right-hand side. The same applies to the lower numbers.
> Atomic numbers (also known as proton numbers) are at the bottom.
> Atomic mass numbers (also known as nucleon numbers) are at the top.

Total: 12 Foundation level marks + 4 additional Higher level marks

7. (a) (i) the two parts of the strip have the same charge and therefore repel each other*

    (ii) the two parts of the strip will be attracted to his hand*

> **TIP**
> This part of the question doesn't ask for a reason, only *what* will happen.

    (iii) the two parts of the strip will be repelled away from the pen so that they are further apart than before*; this is because the strip and the pen will both have the same (negative) charge*

> **TIP**
> This time there was a mark for a reason because the question said *explain*!

    (iv) when the strip was rubbed, electrons were transferred from the cloth to the strip so that it became negatively charged**
     (Since some plastics (but not polythene) can be charged positively, you would be given the marks if you went through all of this answer assuming that the

strips became positive. In this part the electrons would then have been removed on to the cloth.) **6 marks**

(b) The droplets will all have the same charge, so they will repel each other and spread out* into a fine mist. The droplets will then be attracted to the earthed plants, and they will cover both sides of the leaves better.* **2 marks**

(c) John's father could work on an earthed bench (some benches have a metal surface connected to earth by a wire); wear an earthed wrist band or, at least, earth his hands at regular intervals.* (The mark is given for the idea of earthing charges by any suitable method.) **1 mark**

Total: 9 marks

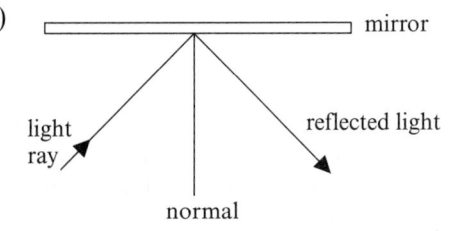

8. (a) (i) The normal should meet the mirror at 90° as shown on the diagram.* **1 mark**

(ii) The ray should be reflected as shown on the diagram.* (It isn't usual to measure the angle with a protractor to check this, it must look as though the angles are equal.) **1 mark**

(iii) angle of incidence = angle of reflection* **1 mark**

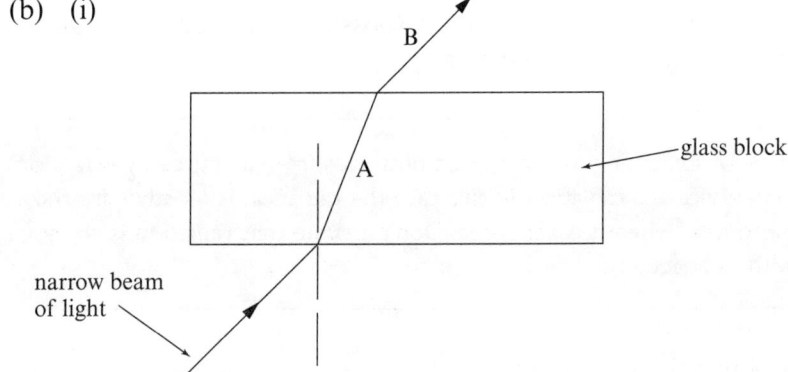

(b) (i) The ray will bend towards the normal as it goes in (see **A** on the diagram)*; then will leave the block by bending away from the normal (see **B** on the diagram) and will therefore be parallel to the direction in which it entered.* **2 marks**

(ii) refraction* **1 mark**
(iii) the wave changes speed as it enters the new material* **1 mark**

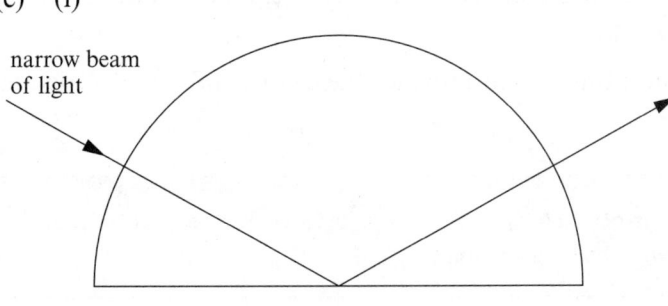

(c) (i) The ray of light will be totally internally reflected as shown in the diagram.* **1 mark**

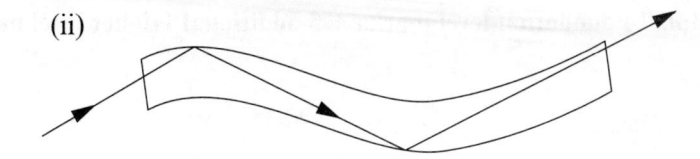

(ii) The ray will reflect along the inside of the glass so that it can follow the bend of the fibre.* **1 mark**

> **TIP**
>
> You will not be penalised for having the wrong number of reflections as long as the reflections look reasonable – i.e. reflect off at an approximately equal angle. You will lose the mark if the reflections are clearly impossible!

    (iii) one from: fibroscopy (medical uses to look inside the throat/lungs/stomach)/ transmission of telephone calls/ cable TV* **1 mark**

Total: 10 marks

9. (a) (i) The ship's captain must use a satellite because the radio waves travel in straight lines, so can't reach the base because of the curve of the earth's surface (see the diagram in the question).* The waves can go to and from the satellite in straight lines. **1 mark**

    (ii) microwaves/radio waves* **1 mark**

    (iii) The satellite has an orbit that is above the equator* and it goes round the earth once every 24 hours*. Because the earth is also spinning on its axis once every 24 hours, the satellite will appear to be stationary above one place when it is really travelling round in its orbit *very* quickly! **2 marks**

(b) (i) The panels are to collect the energy being radiated by the sun and turn it into electricity to keep its batteries charged.*

    (ii) The satellite is a long way above the atmosphere so there is no friction (or 'drag') from the panels* – a spacecraft can be any shape and does not need to be streamlined!

    (iii) The satellite could be wrapped in shiny metal foil (possibly thin gold) that would reflect away the infra-red radiation.* **3 marks**

> **TIP**
>
> You are asked about *radiation*. This is energy being carried outwards from a source by waves or particles. For example, sound waves are radiation. In this case the radiation is mostly infra-red from the sun which turns into heat when it is absorbed. Don't assume that radiation is always dangerous, or confuse it with radioactivity.

***(c) (i) the orbit goes over both poles of the earth*

    (ii) As the earth rotates, the orbit will eventually pass over all of the earth's surface.* (It will pass over a different part of the earth on each orbit.)
Use: one from weather/ inspecting crops/ checking on rainfall/ climate changes/ military uses.* (Note that observing other countries' crops can be as valuable as military information!)

    (iii) the earth attracts the satellite*; this weight provides the centripetal force needed to keep it in orbit.* **5 marks**

> **TIP**
>
> You need to be careful here – there is no such thing as *centrifugal* force, it does not exist and explanations that use such an idea will not be given marks.

Total: 7 Foundation level marks + 5 additional Higher level marks

10. (a) (i)

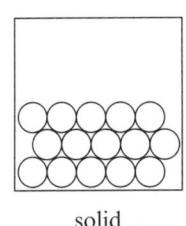

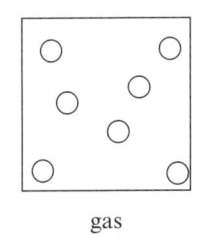

solid — liquid — gas

The liquid will show the particles close together at the bottom of the box, but not in a regular pattern*; the gas will show the particles spaced out much more and spread out over the whole box.* **2 marks**

(ii) the gas* (iii) the solid* (iv) the gas* **3 marks**

> **TIP**
> Don't be put off by the fact that the answer for (iv) is the same as that for (ii) – the question does NOT say that you have to use each possible answer once.

(v) The gas particles were dissolved in the liquid* which keeps them all closely packed together. When the gas bubble forms, the particles in the gas will be MUCH further apart so that the bubble takes up a lot more space and is seen more easily* **2 marks**

(b) (i) A* (ii) C* (iii) D* **3 marks**

> **TIP**
> Don't assume that all questions get harder as you go through them. This bit looks difficult but is probably the easiest part of the question!

(c) (i) The particles in the liquid fit into a smaller space* so that the cylinder can hold more fuel than if it was all gas – it is also less dangerous than having a very high pressure of gas in a cylinder. **1 mark**

(ii) Energy is needed to change the liquid into a gas* and this energy is taken from the surroundings which become colder*. The energy transferred is called latent heat.
2 marks

***(iii) energy transferred = 4200 × mass × rise in temperature*
= 4200 × 0.5 × 70
= 147 000 J (= 147 kJ)* **2 marks**

> **TIP**
> You don't need to have memorised this equation to be able to do the question! You are told that each 1 kg takes 4200 J for a 1 °C change. If you only have 0.5 kg then it will only take 0.5 times as much energy. If you raise the temperature by 70 °C instead of 1 °C then it should take 70 times as much energy.

$$\text{power} = \frac{\text{energy transferred*}}{\text{time taken}}$$

$$= \frac{147\,000}{15 \times 60} \quad \text{(Don't forget to change the time to seconds.)}$$

= 163 W* **2 marks**
(No marks for the units for the answers this time as they are given in the question.)

Total: 13 Foundation level marks + 4 additional Higher level marks

Total marks for this paper = 113 for the Foundation level or 137 if you did the Higher level.

Solutions to Paper 2

1. (a) (i) north* (ii) they will attract each other* (iii) iron*
    (iv) aluminium cans will have no effect on the compass needle* **4 marks**

    > **TIP** Poles that are the same repel and opposite poles attract. Except for nickel and cobalt, the other metals are non-magnetic.

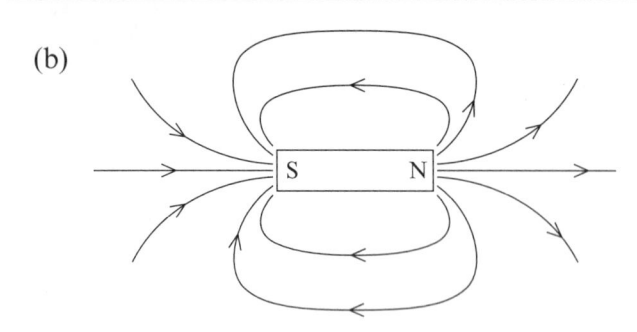

    (b)

    [Diagram of magnetic field lines around a bar magnet with S on left and N on right]

    **   **2 marks**

    (c) (i) the electromagnet will **repel** one end of the needle*

    > **TIP** You will not get marks if you say that the needle is attracted. The nail will be attracted to the needle even when the current in the coil is turned off!

    (ii) more turns on the coil*/ more current*
    (Note – the size of the nail has no real effect on the strength of the magnet.)

    (iii) the new magnet will be MUCH weaker* **4 marks**

    (d) (i) switch off the current*

    (ii) the poles continuously swap over*
    (Note – it doesn't matter since either pole attracts the iron!)

    (iii) The magnet only attracts the iron and leaves behind other metals and non-metals so that a simple sorting has been done.* **3 marks**

    Total: 13 marks

2. (a) The speed of sound is *much* slower than the speed of light.* **1 mark**

    (b) distance = speed × time taken*
    = 340 × 3
    = 1020 m (= 1.02 km)* **2 marks**

    (c) (i) ultrasound* (ii) body scans instead of X-rays/ cleaning delicate objects*

    (iii) frequency is the number of waves per second* (iv) hertz / Hz* **4 marks**

    Total: 7 marks

3. (a) Put some water into a measuring cylinder and note the volume.*
    Put the ball bearing carefully into the cylinder and note the new reading for the volume of water.*
    Subtract the first reading from the second.* **3 marks**

    > **TIP** You can describe *any* suitable method as long as you state clearly both what you DO and what you MEASURE.

(b) density = $\dfrac{\text{mass}}{\text{volume}}$ *

$= \dfrac{11.2}{1.4} = 8$ g/cm³ *   **2 marks**

> **TIP**
> The equation for this calculation was given at the start of the exam papers – did you check that you had got it right?

(c) The paper has a bigger area and will therefore have more air resistance at the same speed. Since this 'drag' force acts upwards, it cancels some of the downward force (the weight) and the paper accelerates downwards more slowly.*   **1 mark**

Total: 6 marks

4. (a) galaxy*; the Milky Way*; light years*; away from us*; red*; solar system*; gravity*   **7 marks**

   (b) (i) Mars* (ii) Pluto* (iii) 258 200 h* (iv) 5800 h* (v) 3900 N*   **5 marks**

   (vi) Mercury is much closer to the Sun and therefore receives more energy per sq metre at its surface.*   **1 mark**

   ***(vii) The gases will absorb some of the radiation that is sent out by the planet* and radiate it back towards the planet so that the heat energy becomes 'trapped' and the temperature rises.* On Earth we call this the 'greenhouse effect'.   **2 marks**
   (You might get one mark for saying that the gases behave like a blanket and trap the heat in, but it is not very scientific!)

   (c) (i) any one of: much smaller/ made of ice/ orbit is a much bigger ellipse/ orbit is at an angle to the plane of the orbits of the other planets*   **1 mark**

   (ii) gravity*   B is closer to the Sun*   **2 marks**

Total: 16 Foundation level marks + 2 additional Higher level marks

5. (a)

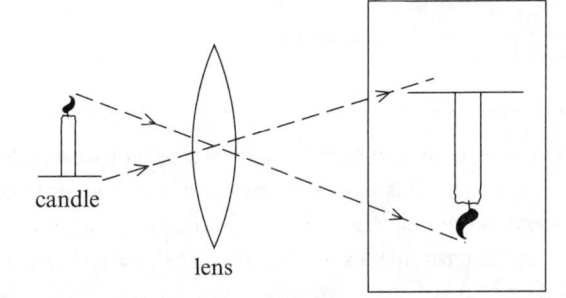

The diagram should show that the image is inverted (upside down)* and that the image is bigger than the object.*   **2 marks**

> **TIP**
> The best way to find the correct place for the image is to draw straight rays passing through the centre of the lens, as shown on the diagram.

(b) (i) closer to the lens* (ii) becomes smaller*   **2 marks**

(c) She could use the lens to produce a sharp focused image of a **distant** object on a screen* and then measure the distance from the lens to the screen.*   **2 marks**

> **TIP**
> You should note that the question says *approximate*, there is only a small space, and there are only two marks. The method must therefore be a simple and short one. If you do write about a longer, more accurate and 'better' method, there will still only be two marks! This is a good example of where the spacing on the paper helps.

(d)

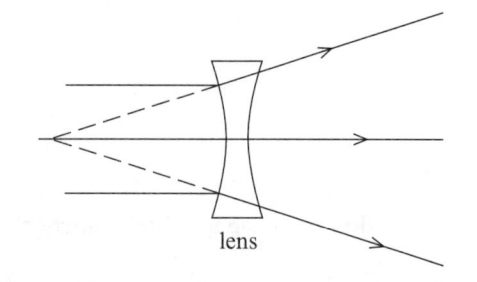

(i) The three rays should diverge* away from a common point (focus)* **2 marks**

(ii) Correction of short sight/ eyepiece in some optical instruments* **1 mark**

Total: 9 marks

6. (a) field*; induced/produced/made*; induction* **3 marks**

   (b) (i) galvanometer*

> **TIP**
> Sometimes you can get a mark by describing what is needed even if you have forgotten the exact name. In this case you could get a mark by saying that the meter must be one that can measure small currents.

   (ii) there will be a zero reading, no current or voltage produced*

   (iii) the reading will be larger* and in the opposite direction*

   (iv) the readings will be larger* **5 marks**

   (c) (i) the 'mains' supply is 230 V. This is too large and will damage any transistors or diodes in the circuit.* **1 mark**
   (Note that the question asks WHY and therefore just saying that the voltage is too big is not really a satisfactory answer. It is possible for your answer to be true but not to be worth marks!)

   (ii) secondary voltage = primary voltage × $\dfrac{\text{number of turns on secondary coil}}{\text{number of turns on primary coil}}$

   = $230 \times \dfrac{180}{4600}$* = 9 V * **2 marks**

> **TIP**
> The equation for this will usually be given (you should check your own syllabus carefully so that you know which equations you have to learn). In this case the equation is at the start of the exam papers, in the information – did you remember; did you check that you had the equation correct? Because the equation is given to you, the marks are for the working and the answer rather than for the equation.

   (iii) iron* **1 mark**

   (iv) The d.c. would make a constant magnetic field; the field must be changing for a voltage to be induced.* **1 mark**

***(d) A is a diode/rectifier*; it lets current through in only one direction*
B is a capacitor*; it stores some charge to smooth out the voltage* **4 marks**

Total: 13 Foundation level marks + 4 additional Higher level marks

7. (a) (i) Black (dark, matt) surfaces are best at absorbing the radiated energy.* **1 mark**

   (ii) insulation to avoid heat energy being lost from the hot water to the surroundings*; the higher pipe will carry the warmer water* **2 marks**

> **TIP**
> You can work this out by thinking about a convection current as the water is heated in the panel.

(iii) Either the pipes will be made from copper* BECAUSE a metal is needed for strength / iron would rust*
or the pipes are made from plastic* BECAUSE this material is a better insulator*
2 marks
(The first mark for choosing a material is only given when you also have a good, scientific, reason for choosing it.)

(iv) No energy will have been absorbed overnight, so the water will have cooled (or the hot water used and not replaced).* **1 mark**

(v) The darker surface will be a better absorber of radiation.* **1 mark**

(vi) If the blinds are pulled down during the day, they will reflect away a lot of the radiation that would pass through the windows and be absorbed inside the caravan – the silver surface reflects infra-red radiation.* **1 mark**

(b) (i) the gas is a good insulator*; it is trapped in the solid plastic*, so making the walls of the box a good insulator **2 marks**

(ii) The lid is a tight fit so that no air gets in or out and this stops convection currents.*
1 mark

(iii) The bottom of the inside of the box will be coldest* because the cold air will be more dense and will sink to the bottom.* **2 marks**

(c) (i) power = volts × amps*

1200 = 230 × amps

amps = $\overline{\frac{1200}{230}}$ = 5.21 A*

This will mean that the drier cannot be used on the 3 A supply (which would probably be switched off by the circuit breaker that is there to prevent overloads).* **3 marks**

> **TIP**
> The question does say that you should show your working. This is so that the examiner can give you as many marks as possible – even if you make a mistake. You might get at least one mark for just starting with the correct equation.

***(ii) An ELCB (Earth Leakage Circuit Breaker) or RCCB (Residual Current Circuit Breaker)*; will switch off current if an earth current is detected* **2 marks**

(d) (i) moment = force × distance to pivot*
= 750 × 5
= 3750 Nm* **2 marks**
(No mark for the unit here as it is given on the paper)

(ii) move things in the caravan from near the front to closer to the wheels* (so that the turning moment is smaller) **1 mark**

(e) a greater mass needs a greater force to get the same acceleration.* **1 mark**

Total: 20 Foundation level marks + 2 additional Higher level marks

8. (a) (i) Light Dependent Resistor* **1 mark**

(ii) The meter will show a larger current* because the LDR has less resistance in brighter light.* **2 marks**

(b) (i) The voltmeter reading increases.* As the light increases, the resistance of the LDR gets less so it will get a smaller share of the voltage, leaving a bigger share for the resistor.* **2 marks**

(ii) V = IR *
= 0.0050 × 1000 *
= 5 V * **3 marks**

TIP
It does not matter if the equation is in standard symbols or words. This is usually true but you MUST be using the same standard symbols as everybody else!

(c) (i) X = NOT* Y = NOT* Z = AND* **3 marks**

TIP
The only gate that has just one input is the NOT gate.

(ii) X reverses/inverts the output of the light gate* to get a signal that is on/high when it is dark instead of when it is light* **2 marks**

(iii) the heater would come on when it was cold and light* **1 mark**

(iv) a thermistor* **1 mark**

(v)

Light sensor	Temperature sensor	Heater
0	0	1	*
0	1	0	*
1	0	0	*
1	1	0

3 marks (6 × ½ mark)

***(vi) NOR* **1 mark**

***(vii) because the gate cannot supply a large current/voltage without being damaged/ it uses the relay to switch a larger current/ voltage on* **1 mark**

***(d) (i) diode*
(ii) protects the logic gates from high voltages* (that might be generated in the coil)
2 marks
Total: 18 Foundation level marks + 4 additional Higher level marks

***9. (i)

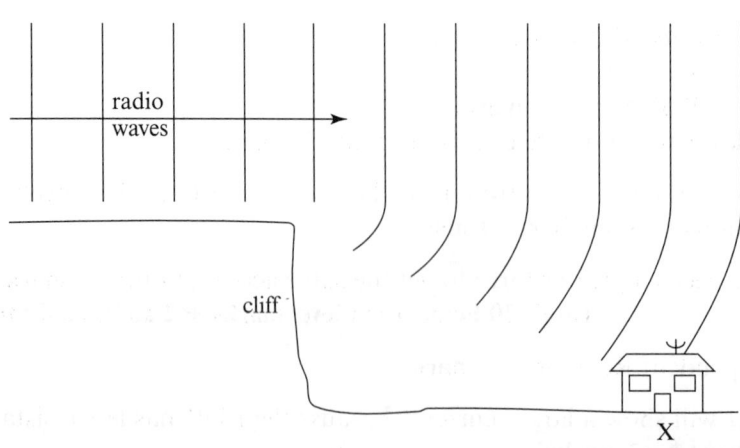

Note that the part of the wave below and after the cliff is being curved downwards*
1 mark

(ii) diffraction* **1 mark**

(iii) The signal gets stronger/louder* because the longer waves are diffracted more.*
2 marks
Total: 4 marks

10. (a) (i) weight = mass × g = 3 × 10 = 30 N*   **1 mark**

> **TIP**
> Even if you don't remember this at first, the question tells you that each 1 kg weighs 10 N so 3 kg must weigh 30 N. You don't need to show the working to get this one mark.

(ii) pressure = $\dfrac{\text{force}}{\text{area}}$*   **1 mark**

(iii) Pressure = $\dfrac{30}{200}$ = 0.15 N/cm²   *answer + *unit   **2 marks**

> **TIP**
> This is a good example of a simple calculation where you will be glad to check your answer with a calculator – make sure that you have it with you!

(b) the force is put on to a very small area at the point of the pin*; so the pressure is big* and the pin goes easily into the board.   **2 marks**

(c) *Either* weight spread out over a bigger area*; so less likely to sink in*
or wider tyres cause lower pressure*; and are less likely to sink into soft ground*   **2 marks**

(d) (i) 100 litres* and method of working, *either* from P1 × V1 = P2 × V2, *or* by saying that making the pressure 20 times smaller will make the volume 20 times bigger*   **2 marks**

(ii) 1 atmosphere*   (iii) 5 litres*   (iv) 95 litres*   **3 marks**

***(e) The pressure of the gas is caused by its particles (molecules) hitting the walls* of the cylinder. Each collision puts a small force on the wall, and there are lots of collisions.*
2 marks

***(f) When the gas inside the can is heated, its pressure rises until the can explodes.* The can is designed to stand higher pressures so it will be more dangerous when it finally explodes.*
2 marks

Total: 13 Foundation level marks + 4 additional higher level marks

Total marks for this paper = 115 for the Foundation level or 135 if you did the Higher level.

Solutions to Paper 3

Section A

1. B	2. B	3. A	4. E	5. B
6. C	7. A	8. D	9. B	10. E
11. C	12. D	13. B	14. B	15. B
16. D	17. C	18. B	19. D	20. B

Total: 20 marks

These multiple choice questions are probably shorter than those you will have in your exams. They are, however, a good way to test a range of facts and can point to the topics that you need to revise a little more before the examinations.

Section B

***21. (a) The radioactivity recorded as the background count is always there, so is not part of the experimental results.* **1 mark**

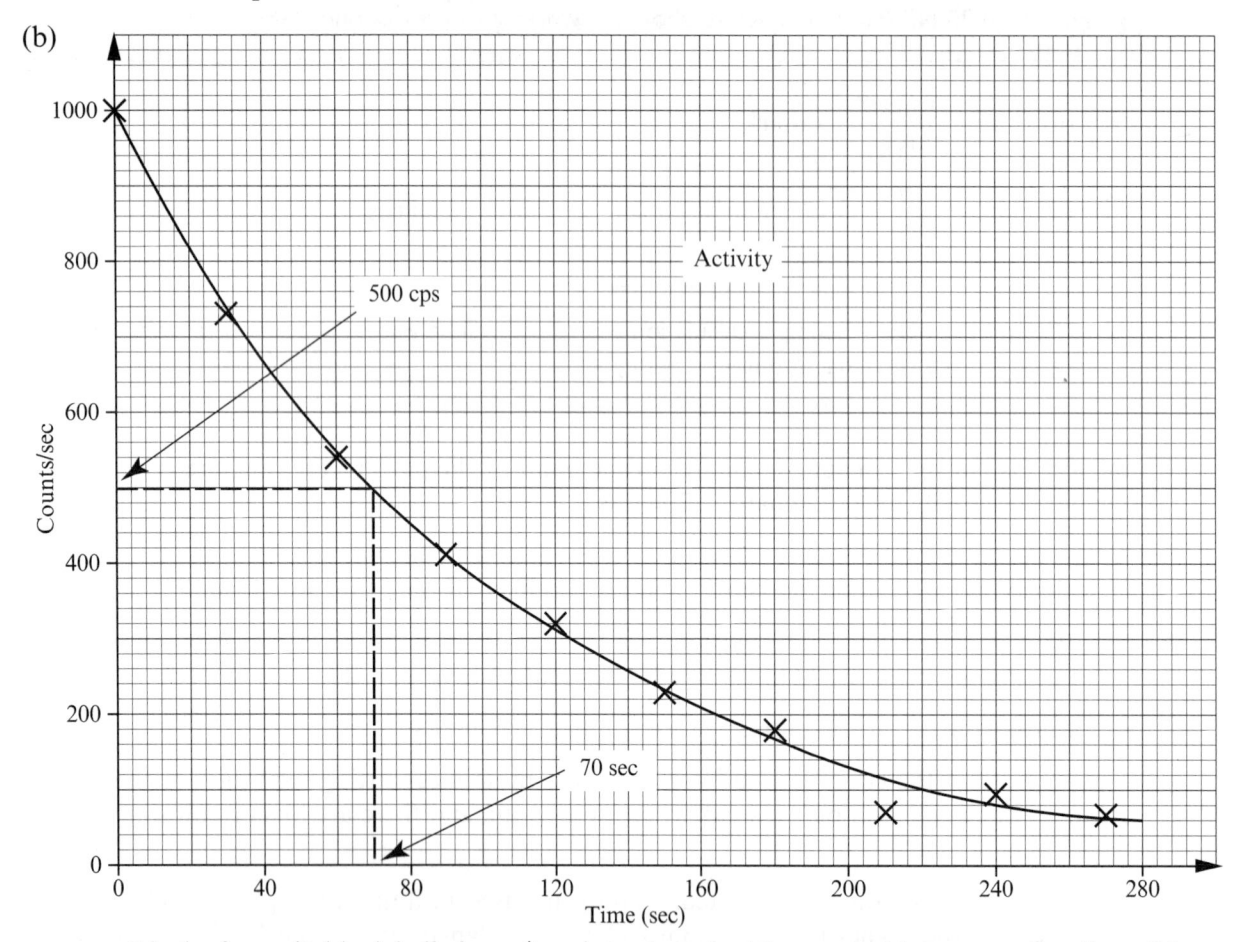

(b)

Marks for: suitable, labelled axes*; points plotted with reasonable accuracy*; a line of best fit* **3 marks**

> **TIP**
> You do not plot this sort of a graph by joining the dots! Put in a 'line of best fit'. This is a smooth curve which goes as close as possible to all of the points. It will miss any points which have an obvious error (usually caused by mistakes in the practical work). It may well be that all the points have small error and that the curve doesn't actually pass through any of them. In exams the examiners are usually reasonable people who make sure that most if not all of the points are right on the line.

(c) The points are not on a smooth curve* Ignore points that are clearly not part of the pattern when drawing the line of best fit* **2 marks**

(d) You can show the working as:
1000 Bq to 500 Bq takes 70 s*; 500 Bq to 250 Bq takes another 70 sec*; half-life is 70 s*

or put lines on the graph to show how you found the time for the activity to halve. (See graph.) Half-life from graph = 70 s **3 marks**
(Two of the marks are for showing the working.)

(e) The material has a short half-life so it can be measured easily/ decays away quickly so it is less dangerous; either answer* **1 mark**

Total: 10 marks for Higher level

Solutions to Paper 3 ■ 61

22. (a) chemotherapy/ as a tracer* **1 mark**
    (You are allowed to give a *brief* description if you have forgotten the name of the technique, the name alone will get the mark in this case.)

    (b) any one of: tracing chemicals/ thickness detector/ sterilising fruit or instruments, etc.*
    1 mark
    Total: 2 marks

23. (a) OR* **1 mark**

    TIP
    Remember that the names of logic gates describe what they do, so this one comes on when **either** of the inputs is on. Remember that the names are in CAPITAL letters.

    (b) The gate can only deal with a low voltage/low current. The relay lets it control a large voltage/current.* **1 mark**
    Total: 2 marks

24. (a) the light will be refracted/leave the glass* **1 mark**

    (b) all of the light is reflected inside the glass* **1 mark**

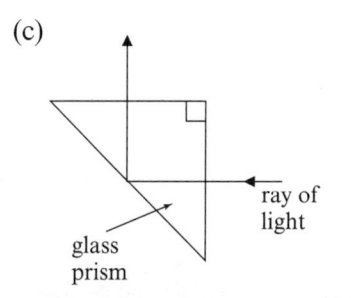

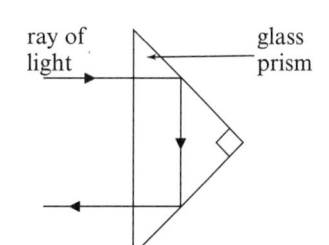

    (c) **There is one mark for each of the correct diagrams – note that the rays are being turned by 90° and 180°. **2 marks**

    (d) (i) binoculars*   (ii) all the light is reflected, so the image is brighter/the binoculars are made much shorter than a telescope* **2 marks**
    Total: 6 marks

25. (a) (i) use glass fibre/mineral wool/mineral pellets, etc.* **1 mark**

    TIP
    Take care not to repeat the question here. It is not good enough to say that you would use roof insulation as it tells you that in the question.
    In the second part, the question asks you how the material works so concentrate on what makes it a good insulator.

    (ii) The material contains a lot of air which is a good insulator.* **1 mark**

    (b) Any one of: walls/ windows/ floor*; with a matching explanation: cavity wall insulation/ double glazing/ carpets* **2 marks**
    Total: 4 marks

26. (a) (i) A battery*; B buzzer*; C motor*; D switch* **4 marks**

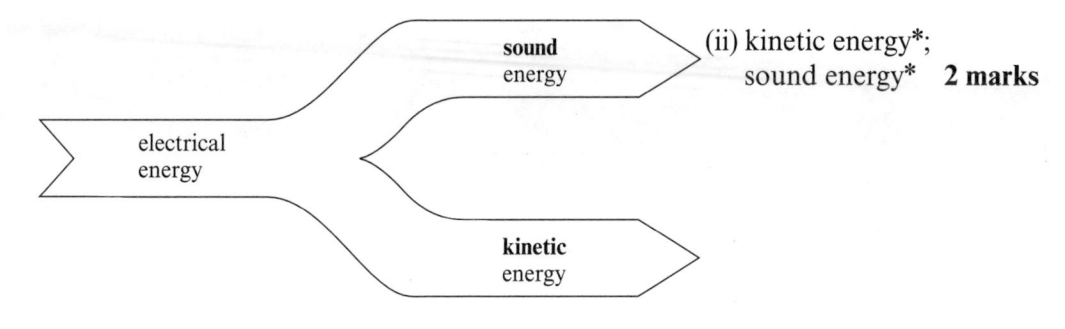

    (ii) kinetic energy*; sound energy* **2 marks**

(iii) $Q = I \times t$*
$= 2 \times 3 \times 60 = 360$ C (= 360 coulombs) answer* unit* **3 marks**

(iv) 0.25 A* **1 mark**

(b) (i) less than 2 A* **1 mark**

(ii) C also stops working* because current would have to pass through *both* B and C for them to work* **2 marks**

(c) (i) $R = \dfrac{V}{I}$*

$= \dfrac{3}{0.5} = 6\ \Omega$ answer* unit* **3 marks**

(ii) $E = V \times I \times t$*
$= 3 \times 0.5 \times 60 = 90$ J answer* unit* **3 marks**

Total: **19 marks**

Total marks for this paper = 53 for the Foundation level or 63 if you did the Higher level.

How well did you do?

Paper 1

Total marks for this paper = 113 for the Foundation level or 137 if you did the Higher level.

Mark	Comment
More than 100	Excellent. Keep up the good work!
More than 80	Very good. You obviously have some ability. Have you revised as much as you can?
More than 60	Good. With more effort you can get into the higher grades.
More than 40	Shouldn't you be doing better? Students who get this many marks can usually get quite a lot more when they make an honest effort.
More than 20	Disappointing. Have a think about how big an effort you are making – is it enough? This is your future!
Less than 20	Either you haven't revised yet or you need help with how to revise properly.

Paper 2

Total marks for this paper = 115 for the Foundation level or 135 if you did the Higher level.

Mark	Comment
More than 110	You're becoming a star!
More than 100	Excellent. Keep up the good work!
More than 80	Very good. You obviously have some ability. Have you revised as much as you can?
More than 60	Good. With more effort you can get into the higher grades. Did you answer all of the questions? Did you lose some marks because you didn't check your paper?
More than 40	Shouldn't you be doing better? Students who get this many marks can usually get quite a lot more when they make an honest effort. Start to make a big effort in the topics where you got the lowest marks.
More than 20	Disappointing. Have a think about how big an effort you are making – is it enough? This is your future!
Less than 20	Either you haven't revised yet or you need help with how to revise properly.

Paper 3

Total marks for this paper = 53 for the Foundation level or 63 if you did the Higher level.

Mark	Comment
***More than 50	Another good mark! Check where you lost marks. Make sure that you are not wasting marks that would get you a higher grade by missing out simple things like units.
More than 40	Better than average! Still some polishing to be done?
More than 20	You obviously know some facts but you need to spend more time on revision.
Less than 20	You have a lot of revision still to do. Make sure you can pick up the easy marks that you can get by learning the equations.

With any luck you will have done most of your revision by now and you will find a lot of these questions quite easy. Get into the habit of having a go at **all** of the questions – it is surprising how many marks you can pick up – even if you have to leave the harder ones and come back to them later.

the rembrandts
L.P.

Project Manager: Jeannette DeLisa
Photography: Caroline Greyshock

© 1995 WARNER BROS. PUBLICATIONS
All Rights Reserved

Any duplication, adaptation or arrangement of the compositions
contained in this collection requires the written consent of the Publisher.
No part of this book may be photocopied or reproduced in any way without permission.
Unauthorized uses are an infringement of the U.S. Copyright Act and are punishable by law.

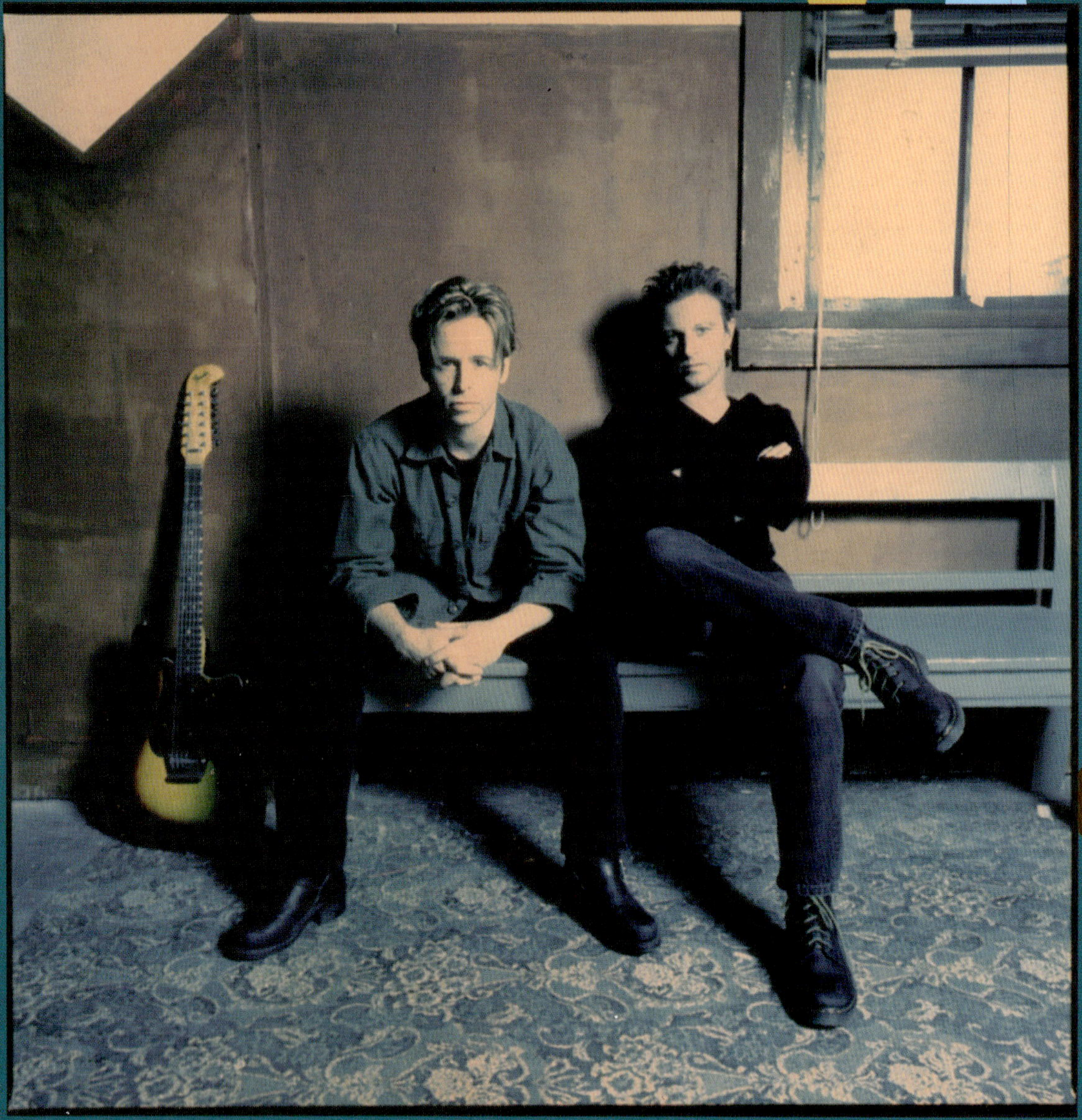

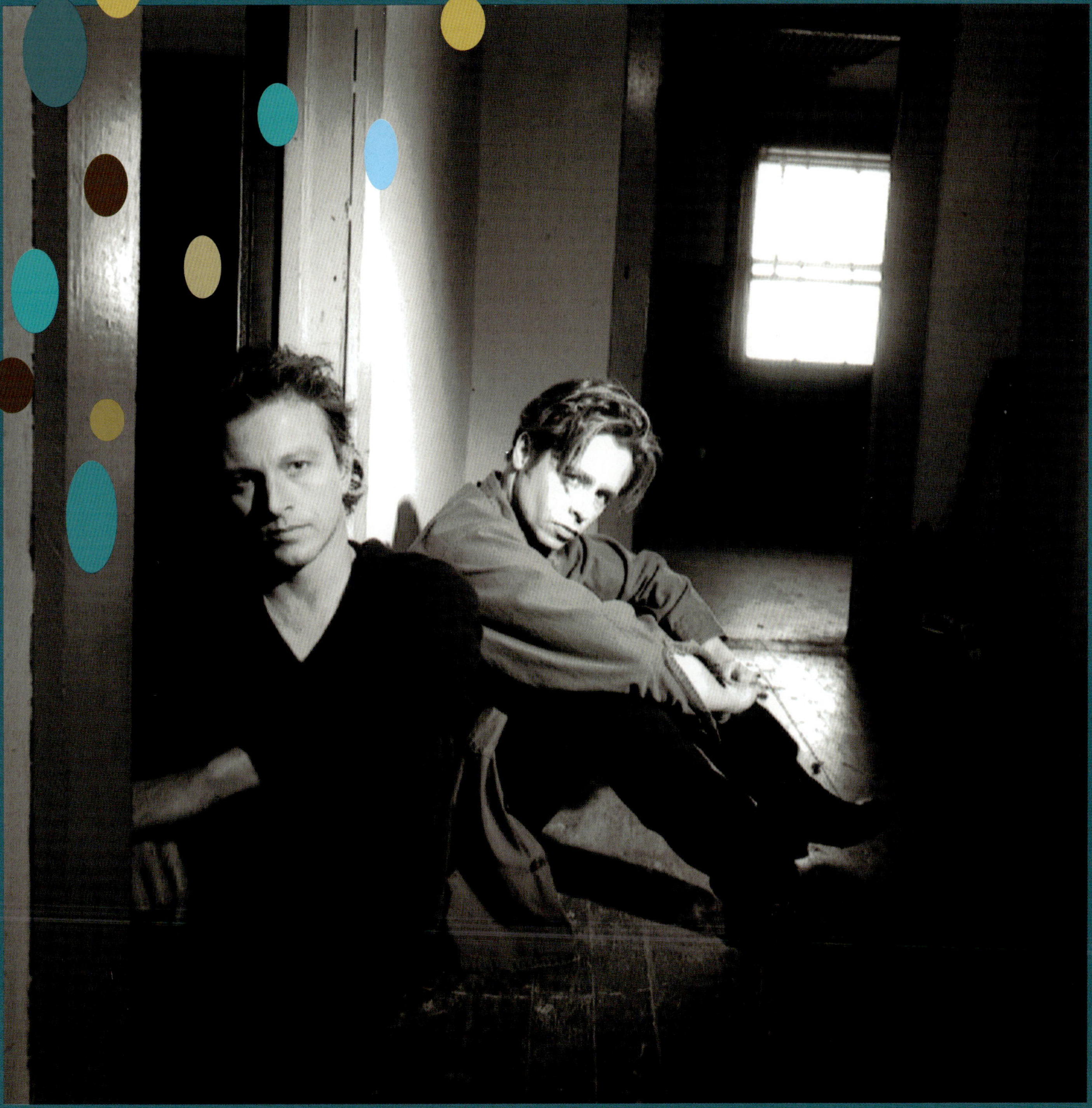

L.p.

the rembrandts

Long Player

contents

40. April 29
24. As Long As I Am Breathing
45. Call Me
55. Comin' Home
67. Don't Hide Your Love
60. Drowning In Your Tears
50. Easy To Forget
36. End Of The Beginning
6. I'll Be There For You (Theme from "Friends")
18. Lovin' Me Insane
76. My Own Way
72. The Other Side Of Night
83. There Goes Lucy
12. This House Is Not A Home
30. What Will It Take

I'LL BE THERE FOR YOU
(Theme from "FRIENDS")

Words by
David Crane, Marta Kauffman, Allee Willis,
Phil Solem and Danny Wilde

Music by
Michael Skloff

Fast rock ♩ = 190

C♯m
G
love life's D. O. A.
things are go - ing great.
(1.3.) It's like you're al - ways stuck in sec - ond gear.
(2.) Your moth - er warned you there'd be days like these.
Bm
A
Well, it hasn't been your day, your week, your month, or e - ven your
But she did n't tell you when the world has brought you down to your
G
D/F♯
Esus
1.2.
To Next Strain
E
year. But
knees, that
3.
year.
Chorus:
A
D
E
I'll be there for you when the

*Guitar fill reads 8va.

I'll Be There for You - 6 - 3

er know — me,
no one could ev - er see — me.
F♯m
Seems you're the on - ly one — who knows — what it's
like to be — me.
Bm
Some - one to face — the day — with,
D/A
make it through all — the rest — with,
G
some - one I'll al -

ways laugh with. E-ven at my worst, I'm best with you. Yeah!

(1st time only)
(Inst. solo ad lib....

...end solo)

To Coda ⊕ *D.S. al Coda*

Coda
Chorus:
A
D
I'll be there for you
E
A
I'll be
D
E
there for you
A
D
E
I'll be there for you 'cause you're
D/F♯
G
A
there for me, too.
*

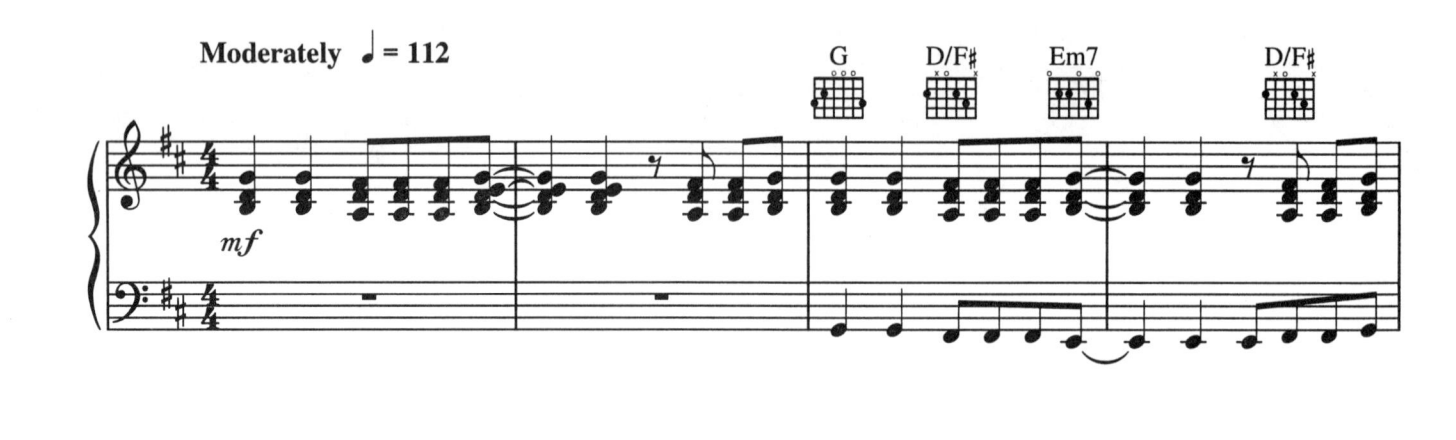

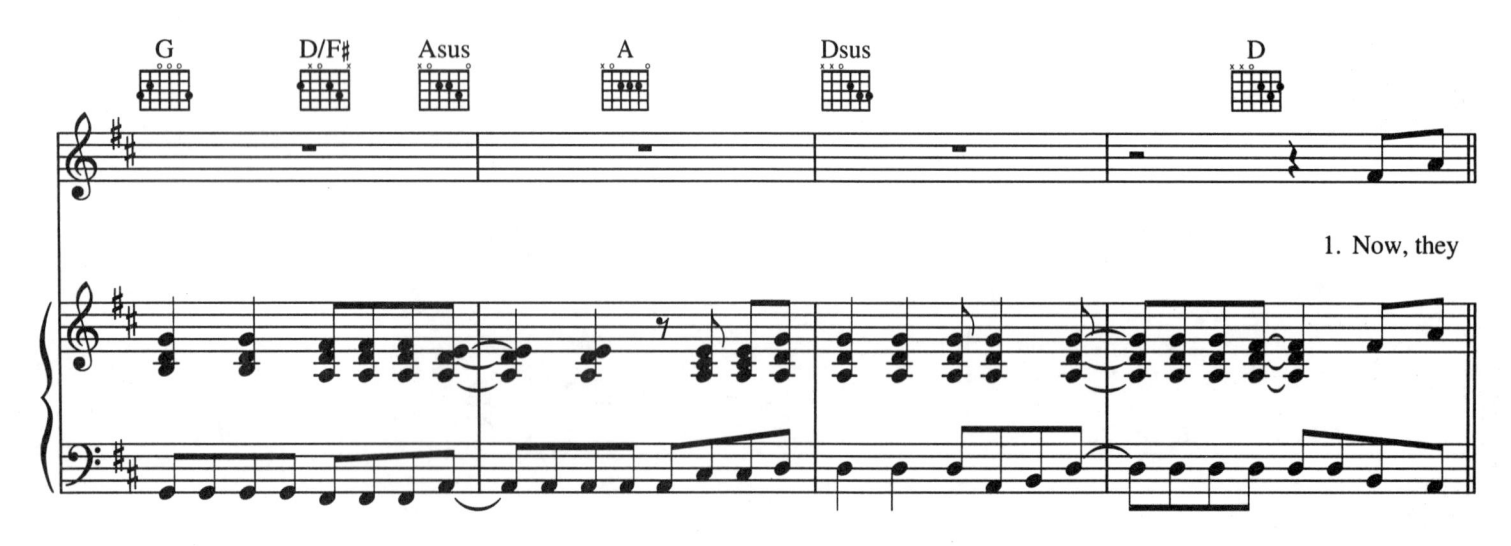

THIS HOUSE IS NOT A HOME

Words and Music by
Phil Solem and Danny Wilde

1. Now, they

Verse:
say a man___ ain't sup-posed_ to cry,___ then
mean to say,___ is that I need_ you now,___ and I'm

why do I have tears in my eyes? If I were
sor-ry if I hurt you some-how. So if it's

half as strong as the steel-y sun, then I
in your heart, you will come back to me, and we could

could mend what I have un-done. No, this house
get it back the way it should be.

Chorus:

__ is not__ a__ home,__ no,__ this house__ is not__ a__ home,__

__ no,__ this house__ is not__ a__ home__ with-out you.__

2. And what I

This House Is Not a Home - 6 - 3

Bridge:

Lyrics:
And with God as my witness, this I swear to you, and with my heart, I do pro-

This House Is Not a Home - 6 - 4

-mise, I__ will love__ and hon-or you.__

3. So if it's __ with-out you.__

No,__ this house__ is not a__ home,__

This House Is Not a Home - 6 - 5

no,___ this house___ is not___ a___ home,___ no,___ this house___ is not___ a___ home___ with - out you.___

With-out you,___ with-out you,_____ with-out you,_____ with-out you._____

LOVIN' ME INSANE

Words and Music by
Phil Solem and Danny Wilde

Moderately fast ♩ = 128

%o Verse:

1.4. Some - bod - y wake__
2. You're un - der - neath__
3. *Instrumental*

Lovin' Me Insane - 6 - 1

© 1995 WB MUSIC CORP., WARNER-TAMERLANE PUBLISHING CORP.,
W3705 MUSIC and ONE HUNDRED BILLION DOLLAR MUSIC
All Rights on behalf of W3705 MUSIC Administered by WB MUSIC CORP. (ASCAP)
All Rights on behalf of ONE HUNDRED BILLION DOLLAR MUSIC Administered by
WARNER-TAMERLANE PUBLISHING CORP. (BMI)
All Rights Reserved

— me up,— some - bod - y talk— me down,— some - bod - y help—
— my feet,— you know where I— will go— be - fore I get—

— me.
— there.

I'm crash - ing in— the clouds,— I'm
You track my ev - ery move,— you're

fall - ing from__ the moon,__ some - bod - y help__ me.
mess - in' with__ my groove__ more than I can__ bear.

Chorus:

I'm go - ing cra-

-zy,__ you're driv - ing me__ mad. You're

E7(♯9)
A5
Adim7
A5
lov - in' me___ in - sane.___
Adim7
A5
Adim7
You're lov - in' me___ in - sane.___
A5
Adim7
4th time to Coda
1.3.
A5
2.
Bridge:
B7(♯9)
I wan - na be in love___ with you,___ I'm gon - na

C
D.S. 𝄋 al Coda
tell you what-cha got - ta do. You got - ta leave it on the oth - er side.
𝄌 Coda
C♯m
I'm go - ing cra - zy, you're driv - ing me mad.
D
E7(♯9)
A5
Adim7
You're lov - in' me in - sane.
A5
Adim7
A5
Adim7
You're lov - in' me in - sane.

23

AS LONG AS I AM BREATHING

Words and Music by
Phil Solem and Danny Wilde

Slowly ♩. = 42

Verse 1:

1. Now, ba-by, it don't show, but this feel-ing in-side, it fills my world with

As Long As I Am Breathing - 6 - 1

© 1995 WB MUSIC CORP., WARNER-TAMERLANE PUBLISHING CORP.,
W3705 MUSIC and ONE HUNDRED BILLION DOLLAR MUSIC
All Rights on behalf of W3705 MUSIC Administered by WB MUSIC CORP. (ASCAP)
All Rights on behalf of ONE HUNDRED BILLION DOLLAR MUSIC
Administered by WARNER-TAMERLANE PUBLISHING CORP. (BMI)
All Rights Reserved

25

tell it to you a-gain to-night, a-gain to night._____ Don't you know that
sured that I won't run a-way, run a-way._____ Can't you see that
ev - er, 'cause it's the on-ly way, the on-ly way I know.

Chorus:

I'll,___ I'll be your man._____ As long as I'm liv-ing,

by you I'll stand. Ba-by, don't you know I'll,___ I'll be your

D♭
To Coda ⊕
E♭
man, as long as I, as long as I am breath-
1.
F C F C B♭ B♭/C F
ing.
C F Am7 B♭
3. And
2.
F C F C
ing.
B♭ B♭/C F C F Am7 B♭
As long as I am breath - ing.
Oh, as

long as blood is cours-ing through my veins I'm gon-na make it right. This

love will nev - er end. Oh, and as long as we can lift our

heads a - bove the clouds to see the light, this love will

nev - er end. *(Guitar solo ad lib. . . .*

... end solo) 4. Oh, long as I am breath - ing.

As long as I am breath - long as I am breath - ing.

As Long As I Am Breathing - 6 - 6

WHAT WILL IT TAKE

Words and Music by
Phil Solem and Danny Wilde

Moderately ♩ = 102

1. These days sliding off an empty page.
2. funny how nothing ever stays the same.
3. *Instrumental*

Lonely, forever something in our way. But
Helpless, never knowing who's to blame. There
But

What Will It Take - 6 - 1

© 1995 WB MUSIC CORP., WARNER-TAMERLANE PUBLISHING CORP.,
W3705 MUSIC and ONE HUNDRED BILLION DOLLAR MUSIC
All Rights on behalf of W3705 MUSIC Administered by WB MUSIC CORP. (ASCAP)
All Rights on behalf of ONE HUNDRED BILLION DOLLAR MUSIC
Administered by WARNER-TAMERLANE PUBLISHING CORP. (BMI)
All Rights Reserved

deep in__ my soul, your__ light__ is all that__ I'm pray-ing for.__ Sal-
once was__ a time when__ my love was some-thing__ worth fight-ing for.__ Now it's
deep in__ my soul, your__ light__ is all that__ I'm pray-ing for.__ Sal-

va-tion__ is in your eyes,__ but not for me.__
all I__ can do to re-mind you of what could be.__
va-tion__ is in your eyes,__ but not for me.__ What will it take__

Chorus:
__ to make you want__ me, what will it take__ to make__ you mine?__ What would it take__

1.
__ to make you love__ me for__ all__ time? 2. It's

D G C(9) Am7
— to make— you mine?— What would it take— to make you love— me for— all—
Em C(9) Am7
— time? Ba - by, I'd cross— the dark-est val - ley, I would ford—
D/F♯ G C(9) F♯m7 B7
— the riv - er wide,— if that's what it takes— to make you love— me for— all—
Esus C(9) Am7
— time. What would it take?— What would it take.—

What would it take?

Baby, I'd cross the darkest valley, I would ford the river wide, if that's what it takes to make you love me for all time.

rit.

a tempo

END OF THE BEGINNING

Words and Music by
Phil Solem, Danny Wilde and Pat Mastelotto

Verse 1:

1. You_____ were in the cor-ner of my_ eye,_____ and fac-ing out_ in-to the wind, I heard the sound_ of your voice sing-ing._

2. If

Verses 2 & 3:

2. I_____ re-mem-bered where my head has been, I'd let you on_ a se-cret
3. Oh,_____ and in the calm be-fore the storm, the sun is shin-ing dark and

End of the Beginning - 4 - 1

© 1995 WB MUSIC CORP., WARNER-TAMERLANE PUBLISHING CORP.,
W3705 MUSIC, ONE HUNDRED BILLION DOLLAR MUSIC and POPPY-DUE MUSIC
All Rights on behalf of W3705 MUSIC Administered by WB MUSIC CORP. (ASCAP)
All Rights on behalf of ONE HUNDRED BILLION DOLLAR MUSIC and POPPY-DUE MUSIC
Administered by WARNER-TAMERLANE PUBLISHING CORP. (BMI)
All Rights Reserved

in, but it's the end of the beginning. 1. When
warm, be-hind your eyes my world is spin-ning. 2. And

Bridge:

ev - ery day together runs, it's
ev - ery kiss melts in-to one, this
ev - ery day melts in-to one, it's

all we need, to hang our hearts up-on the sil - ver moon.
fro - zen love becomes a pool, how sweet the wa - ter runs.
all we need, to hang our hearts up-on the sil - ver moon.

(Ooh.

Chorus:

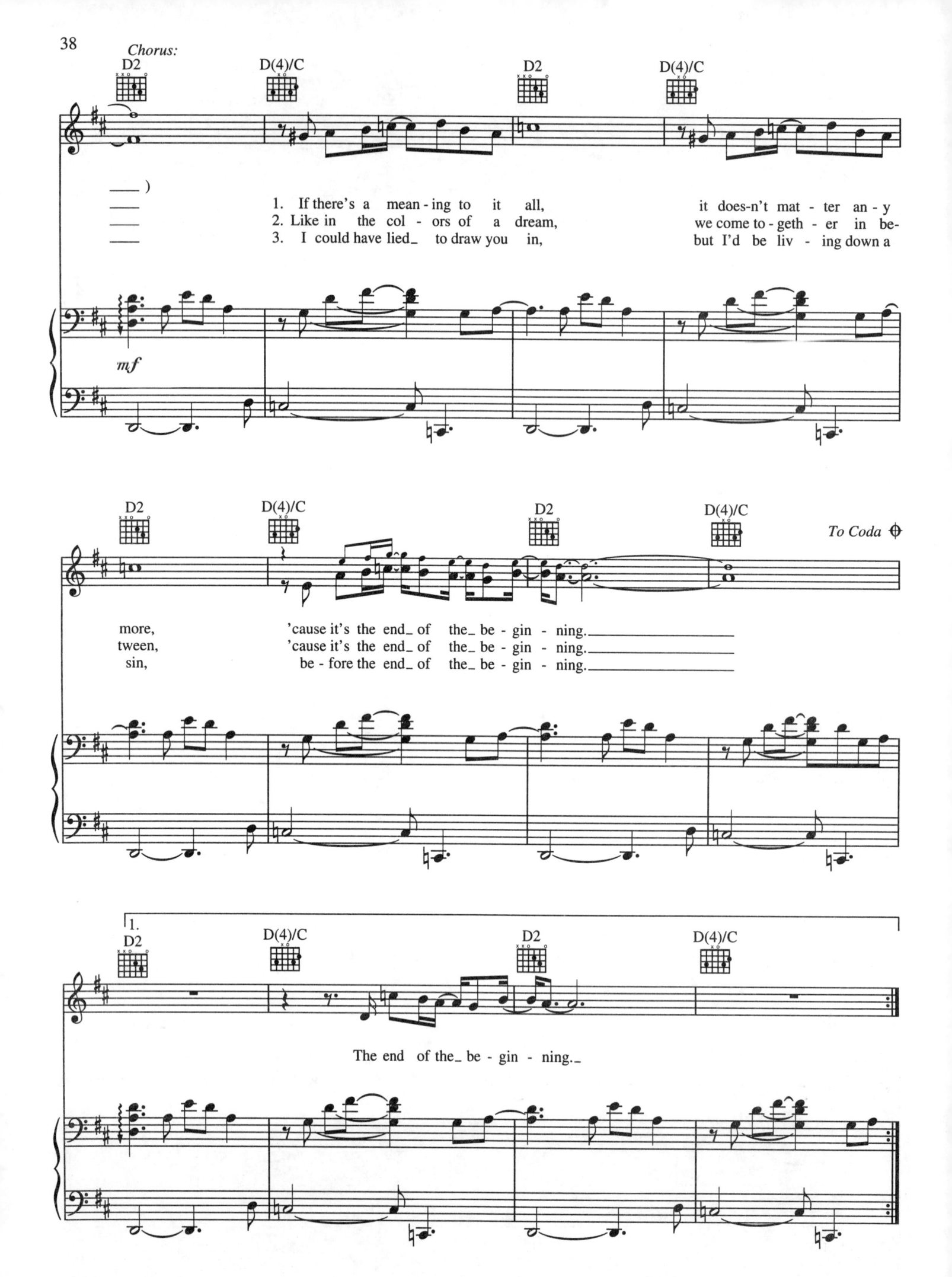

1. If there's a meaning to it all, it doesn't matter any
2. Like in the colors of a dream, we come together in be-
3. I could have lied to draw you in, but I'd be living down a

more, 'cause it's the end of the beginning.
tween, 'cause it's the end of the beginning.
sin,   be-fore the end of the beginning.

1.

The end of the beginning.

2.
D2
D(4)/C
D2
D(4)/C
It's the end_ of the_ be - gin - ning._
D2
D(4)/C
D2
1.2.3.4.
D(4)/C
(Instrumental solo ad lib. . . .
5.
D.S. 𝄋 al Coda
D5
3. And
cresc.
. . . end solo)
Coda
D2
D(4)/C
D2
D(4)/C
Repeat ad lib. and fade
'Cause it's the end_ of the_ be - gin - ning._

APRIL 29

Words and Music by
Phil Solem and Danny Wilde

Moderately slow ♩ = 88

I swear you haven't changed. / and all the foolish things he said. Oh, I called you to tell you / tell me you'll be there, I'm coming home in seven days. / it'll be just like old times. In a word it's all arranged. / April twenty-nine.

Bridge:

I've been so lonely since I lost my mind, and my patience is wearing thin.

But I feel luck-y when I think of you___ and how I'll see your face a-gain.___ *Chorus:* Ev-ery-thing__ is fine, Ap - ril twen-ty - nine.___ I'll try to be__ on time,_____ Ap - ril twen-ty - nine.___

Bm7/E
To Coda
1.
2.
2. I
F♯m
D7/F♯
F♯m
Un-lock the door and throw a-way the key. The sun is shin-ing,
D7/F♯
F♯
D7
E
I'm fin-al-ly free.
F♯
D7
E
B
D.S. al Coda

Coda
D2
C(9)
— Ev - ery - thing_ is fine,
Am7
D2
Bm7/E
D2
Ap - ril twen - ty - nine._
I'll try to be_ on
C(9)
Am7
D2
time, Ap - ril twen - ty - nine._
Bm7/E
D2
Repeat ad lib. and fade
Ev - ery - thing_ is

CALL ME

Words and Music by
Phil Solem, Danny Wilde
and Scott Miller

Moderately ♩ = 104

Verse:

1. We both know you and I have been through harder times.
2. So maybe you were right and maybe I've been wrong.

But now your silence seems a very different kind.
Why did I have to go and wait it out so long?

Bridge:

It feels like I've been
But I didn't mean to

Call Me - 5 - 2

Chorus:

dy - in' just to hear your voice a - gain.
hurt you, if you could on - ly feel my pain.

Call me, call me, can't you hear me cry - in'? Call me, call me, please don't keep me hang - in' on. me hang - in' on.

Call Me - 5 - 3

Verse:

Now, I can't speak for you, I'd wish you'd talk to me.

How diff-i-cult could this one con-ver-sa-tion be?

Chorus:
Call me, call me, can't you hear me cry-in'? Call me, call me, please don't leave me hang-in' on.

Repeat ad lib. and fade

EASY TO FORGET

Words and Music by
Phil Solem and Danny Wilde

Moderate rock ♩ = 120

1. Run, hide from the sun, and fol-low the tracks laid by a thou-sand los-ers' sons who nev-er be-lieved,
2. Fate o-pened the gate, and emp-tied the house dry for an al-i-bi, but you crawled to the edge

who nev-er could read between the lines of love. 1. Do I
and ham-mered a wedge between my heart and soul. 2. Do I

Chorus:
feel bet-ter now. I mean, I think I've got to get you back some-how.
feel bet-ter now. I mean, I wish that I could get you back some-how.
(3.) we know an-y bet-ter now? I mean, I think we've got to get in touch some-how.

I tried to drink you off my mind, but I have-n't yet.

No, you're not eas-y to for-get.
Oh, you're not eas-y to for-get.
Oh, you're not eas-y to for-get.

A7sus
D/A
A7sus
Eas - y to for-get.
A5
A7sus
D/A
To Coda
1.
A7sus
2.
A7sus
cresc.
Bridge:
F♯m
A5
Ba - by, let me take you home,
f
F♯m
A
I've got a rec - ord that I think you used to own.

Ba - by let me take you home, it - 'll be like when we met.

Now is that ea - sy to for - get?

(Instrumental solo ad lib. . . .

. . . end solo)

Ooh, ooh,

ooh.___

3. Do

Coda

Ea - sy to for - get.___

No, you're not ea - sy to for - get.___

Ooh,___ no, you're not ea - sy to for - get.___

COMIN' HOME

Words and Music by
Phil Solem and Danny Wilde

Moderately ♩ = 102

Verse 1:

1. Sit-tin' at the gate, I did-n't have a re-serv-a-tion. Could-n't stand to wait,

Comin' Home - 5 - 1

© 1995 WB MUSIC CORP., WARNER-TAMERLANE PUBLISHING CORP.,
W3705 MUSIC and ONE HUNDRED BILLION DOLLAR MUSIC
All Rights on behalf of W3705 MUSIC Administered by WB MUSIC CORP. (ASCAP)
All Rights on behalf of ONE HUNDRED BILLION DOLLAR MUSIC
Administered by WARNER-TAMERLANE PUBLISHING CORP. (BMI)
All Rights Reserved

Com - in' home, I'm com - in' home, I'm com - in' home to you.

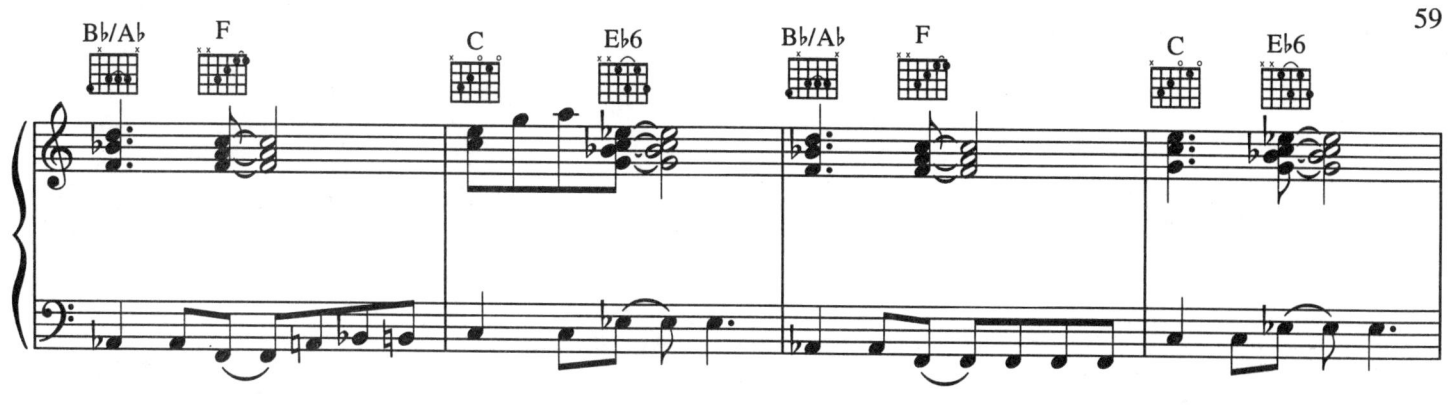

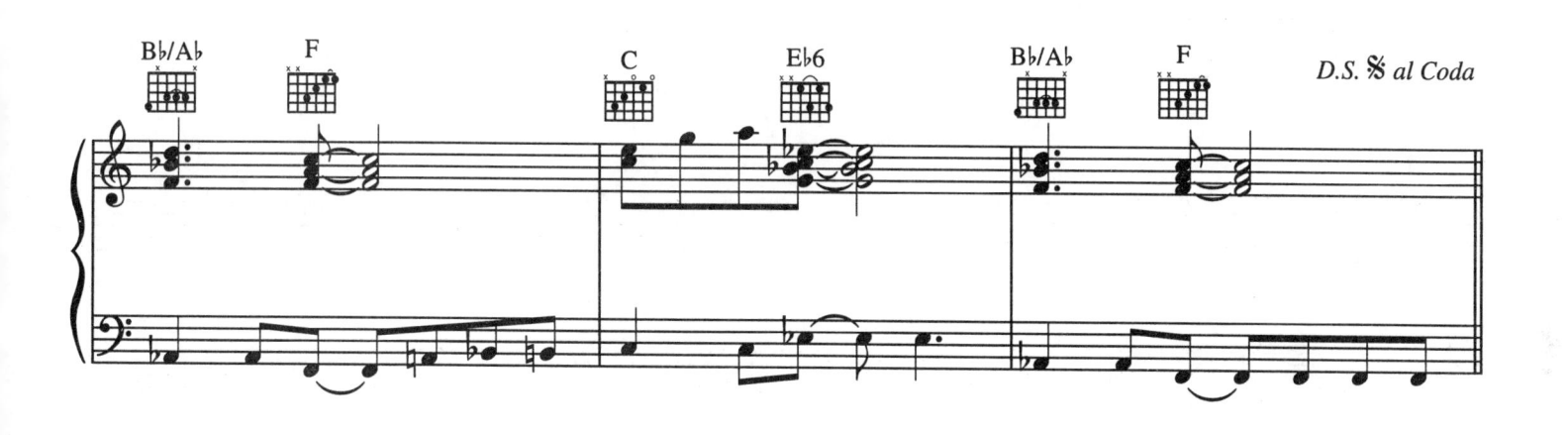

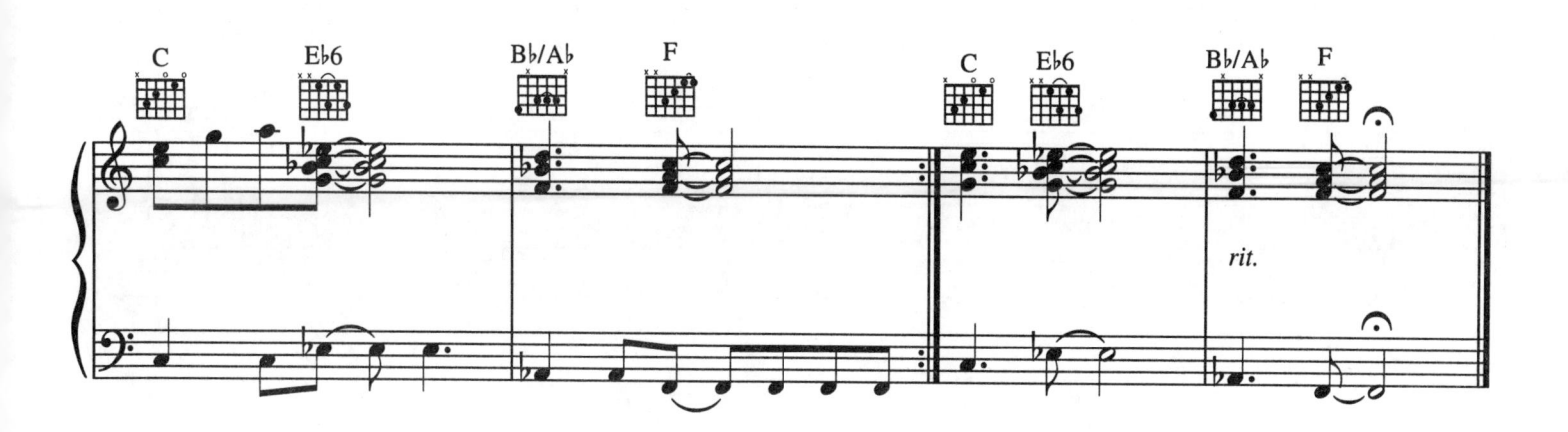

Repeat ad lib. as needed

D.S. 𝄋 al Coda

⊕ *Coda*

rit.

DROWNING IN YOUR TEARS

Words and Music by
Phil Solem, Danny Wilde
and Pat Mastelotto

Moderately ♩ = 92

Drowning in Your Tears - 7 - 2

Chorus:

I'm drown-ing in your tears. Do you rev-el in this pain? I'm drown-ing in your tears; they roll down your face like fall-ing rain.

G/A
A7
2.
C
G/B
like fall - ing rain.
3.
D.S. 𝄋 al Coda
Bridge:
Bm
C
like fall - ing rain.
For - ev - er, you'll be a part of me,
mf
Am
Em
Bm
as sure as the air is ours to breathe.
I'm hop - ing that we
C
Am
B7
will find a way for us to walk on our sep - 'rate ways.

Instrumental solo ad lib. . . .

. . . end solo

Drowning in Your Tears - 7 - 5

C♯m
A(9)
I'm wait - ing for the band to play
F♯m
B7sus
D.S. 𝄋
a song to car - ry me a - way.
cresc.
Coda
C
G/B
like fall - ing rain.
dim.
Gmaj7/A
A7
G/A
A7
mp

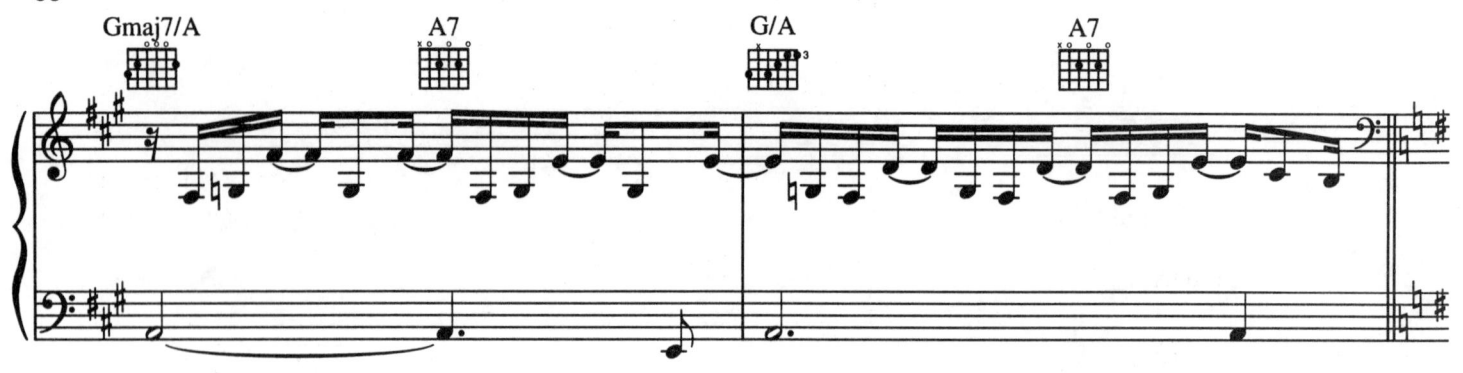

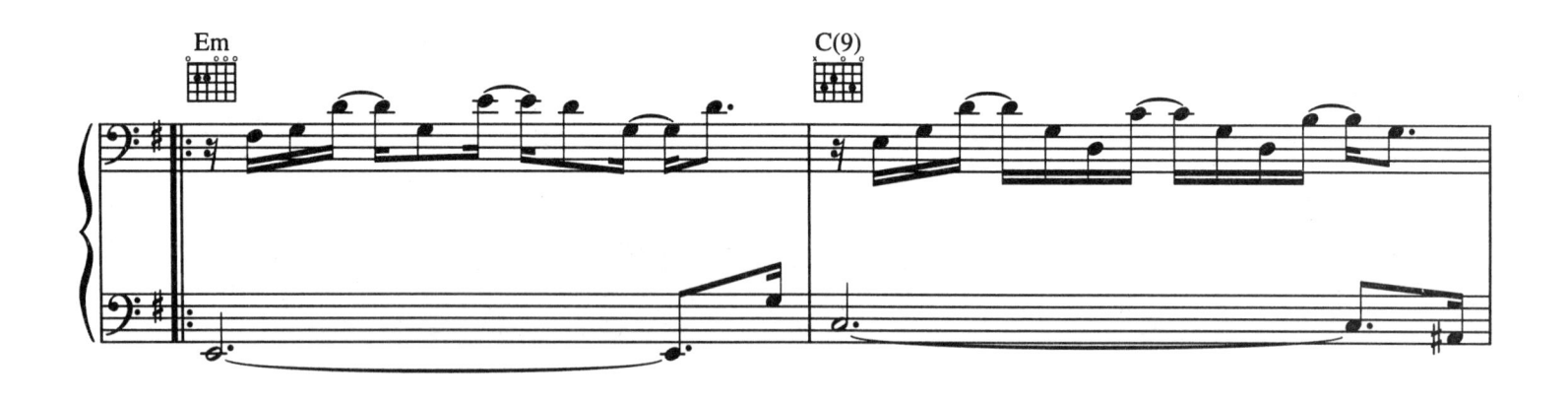

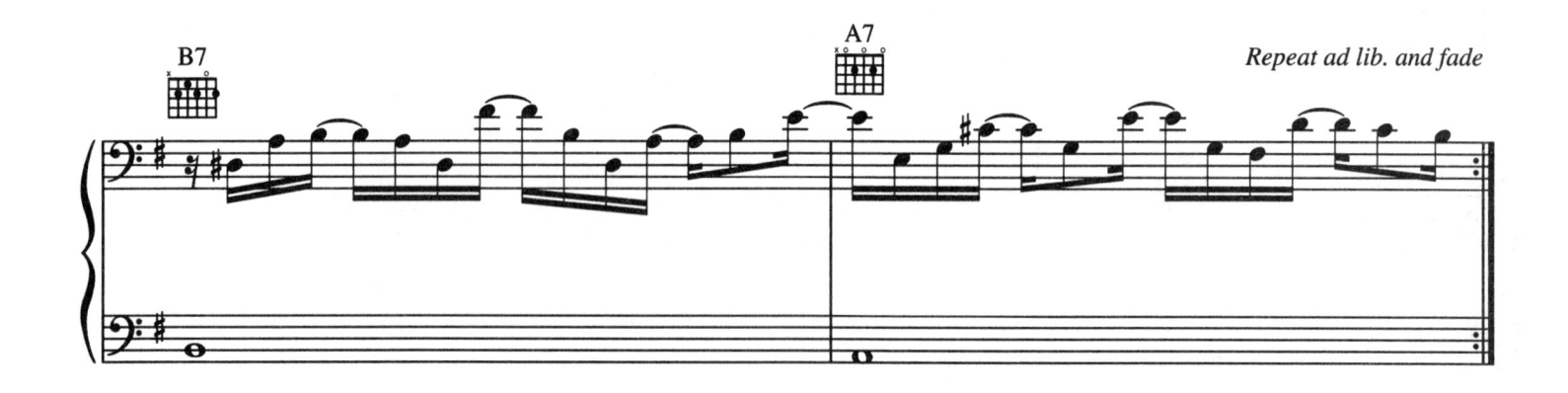

Verse 2:
Now is this all that I live for,
Or is there a door which I have not been through?
Can we go on believing
There's a reason to hold on like we do?
Now what else is there I can say
To make your heartache go away?
(To Chorus:)

DON'T HIDE YOUR LOVE

Words and Music by
Phil Solem and Danny Wilde

Moderate rock ♩ = 100

Verses 1 & 4:

1. There ain't a lot__ that I know,__ but what I do__ goes to show,__
4. *See additional lyrics*

Don't Hide Your Love - 5 - 1

© 1995 WB MUSIC CORP., WARNER-TAMERLANE PUBLISHING CORP.,
W3705 MUSIC and ONE HUNDRED BILLION DOLLAR MUSIC
All Rights on behalf of W3705 MUSIC Administered by WB MUSIC CORP. (ASCAP)
All Rights on behalf of ONE HUNDRED BILLION DOLLAR MUSIC
Administered by WARNER-TAMERLANE PUBLISHING CORP. (BMI)
All Rights Reserved

you know it's nev-er e-nough, oh,_ it's nev-er e-nough.

Verses 2, 3 & 5:

2. I take it in_ and let it out,_ 'cause, ba-by, that's what it's a-bout._
3.5. *See additional lyrics*

Ei-ther I'm in your way, or back in your arms_ a-gain, arms_ a-gain. Let me in,_ yeah.

Chorus:

Don't hide_ your love,_ ba-by, don't hide. Your pride_ is all_

| Dm7 | C(4) | B♭2 | F | Dm7 | G7/B |

that you're think-ing of.___ Don't hide___ your love,_____

| B♭2 | E♭ *To Coda* ⊕ | 1. F | 2. F *To Next Strain* | 3. F *D.S.S. 𝄋 𝄋 al Coda* |

'cause there ain't time e-nough.___

Bridge:

| E♭ | B♭ | Gm7 |

Oh, don't walk a-way;___ I need you to stay.___ You've got to be-lieve___

| D7 | E♭ | B♭ |

___ there's more___ than___ this.___ Oh, how will I know___ if you're let-ting go?___

70

I want what you're want - ing, more or less.

Don't hide your love,

Don't Hide Your Love - 5 - 4

Verse 3:
The same old song in a brand new dress;
I grow so bored, I acquiesce.
Tell me, what can I do to bring you back to me, back to me?
Gonna bring it back, now.
(To Chorus:)

Verse 4:
Today I'm out, tomorrow in.
I'm feeling upside down again.
You know, it's so hard to tell, oh, it's so hard to tell.

Verse 5:
I try to see beyond the rain,
To where we see the light again.
You know, it's here in my heart; it's burning bright for you,
    bright for you.
You gotta bring it home, now.
(To Chorus:)

THE OTHER SIDE OF NIGHT

Words and Music by
Phil Solem and Danny Wilde

Moderately fast ♩ = 120

Verse:

that I could cast would ev - er bring you back too soon.
mov - ing through your wak - ing world, while in my sleep I dream.

1. No spell

A(9)
Emaj7
But still I search_ for hid - den an - swers_ un - der-
You drift as close - ly as_ you can_ with - out you
C♯m9
A(9)
neath this plan_ of view._
ev - er be - ing seen._
The view_
But I
Emaj7
C♯m9
A(9)
_ from here_ should soothe_ my soul,_ e - ven shed some kind_ of light._
know you're there_ be - side_ me, just be - yond my line_ of sight._
know you're out_ there some - where, on - ly you can prove_ me right._
Emaj7
Be - cause I know_ the sun_ is shin - ing_ on the
Up where the sun_ is al - ways shin - ing_ on the
Since you're the one_ who crossed_ the boun - d'ry_ to the

C♯m9
To Coda ⊕ A(9)
oth - er side_ of night,__ on the
oth - er side_ of night,__ on the
oth - er side_ of night,__ to the
Emaj7
oth - er side__ of__ night.
oth - er side__ of__ night.
C♯m9
A(9)
1.
2.
2. Now you're
If you had stayed,_
Bridge:
D(9)
Bm
would I have ev - er found_ a rea - son______

D9
to feel___ this way?___
If you had wait-
Bm
B
D.S. 𝄋 al Coda
-ed one___ more sea - son.___
3.Though I
Coda
A9
Emaj7
on the oth-er side_ of___ night.___
C♯m9
A(9)
Repeat ad lib. and fade
On the oth-er side_ of___ night._

MY OWN WAY

Words and Music by
Phil Solem and Danny Wilde

Verse 1:

You've got to learn how to leave me be for us to ev-er get a-long. You've got to give

77

me the kind of time it takes to prove I'm right or wrong. 'Cause no-bod-y knows what I had to go through, may-be no one e-ven cares. But all the while, as the clock was tick-ing, I've been holed up in my lair, and do-ing things

Chorus 1:

my_____ own way,_____

My Own Way - 7 - 2

my_____ own way._____ You say I don't___

Verse 2:
___ have a leg to stand on, so it's a good___ thing I've___ got two. But if I___ had on-

- ly one leg to stand on, that's ex-act-ly what___ I'd do.___ No one can

(2.) say there's a right or wrong___ way, ev-'ry-one's got___ their own ad-vice.___ Now, am I back___
(3.) one thing on top an-oth-er, and now it's one___ too man-y high.___ I won-der how___

D♯m B D♯m/A♯ G♯7
— to where I start - ed af - ter all — I've sac - ri - ficed — by do-ing things
— man-y piles of things — it takes — to bur - y me — a - live? — I'm do-ing it
cresc.
Chorus 2 & 3:
C♯m A♯dim7 A7 F♯5 G♯5 C♯m A♯dim7
my — own way? —
my — own way. —
My — own way. —
A7 F♯5 E5 C♯m A♯dim7
— Got - ta do things my — own way, —

yeah, my own way.

(Instrumental solo ad lib. . . .)

Verse 3:

3. I've got these feel-ings I'm tryin' to deal with; I'm not so sure you understand that if I seem to be too pre-oc-cu-pied to fit in-to your plans, it's just that it's

D.S. al Coda

My Own Way - 7 - 6

Twice as fast
Coda
A7 F♯5 G♯5 C♯m
I got-ta do things my own way,
(My own way, my
cresc.
ff
A♯dim7 A7 F♯5 G♯5
my own way. I got-ta do things my
own way, my own way, my own way, my own way, my
C♯m A♯dim7 A7
own way, yeah, my own way.
own way, my own way, my own way, my own way, my
1.2.
3.
F♯5 G♯5 F♯5 G♯5 C♯m7
My own way, my own own cra-zy pa-tent-ed way.
own way, my own . . .

THERE GOES LUCY

Words and Music by
Phil Solem, Danny Wilde
and Joe Laswell

Moderately ♩ = 108

Verse:

1. Oh, I see a fal-len an-gel out my bed-room win-dow.
2. here. And Lu-cy says she loves me, just be-cause I'm kind to her.
3. Oh, I see a fal-len an-gel out my bed-room win-dow.

She will find me there, a-mong the used and bro-ken. Take an-oth-er vic-
She will find me there, a-mong the rags and ru-in. I wan-na be a vic-
She takes to the sky, al-though her wing is bro-ken. She's just an-oth-er vic-

To Coda ⊕ [omit 2nd time]

-tim. Who's to say what's fair, do you care? Do you have the an-
-tim.
-tim.

-swer? And who's to say what's love?
Look in-side me, you will find me.

There Goes Lucy - 5 - 2

Chorus:
A(9)
D(9)
A(9)
There goes Lu - cy,
there goes Lu -
D(9)
A(9)
D(9)
- cy, na na na na na.
There goes Lu - cy down my
F♯m7
1.
E
2.
E
street, she's got no-where to go.
But
B
A(9)

E
Esus
E
F♯m7
D.C. al Coda
Coda
D
She in - spires me to re - fine me,
she in - spires me to re - fine me.
A(9)
D(9)
A(9)
There goes Lu - cy, there goes Lu -

D(9)
A(9)
D(9)
- cy, na na na na na. There goes Lu - cy down my
F♯m7
1.
E
2.
E
street, she's got no-where to go. But
A(9)
D(9)
A(9)
here. She's got no-where to go.
D(9)
A(9)
D(9)
rit.
A6
She's got no-where to go. I said she's got no-where to go.
rit.

biography
the Rembrandts

The Rembrandts' aptly titled third album LP, flows from the opening chords of the spiraling first track, "The End Of The Beginning." The duo prefers to get right to work at attacking the senses. The song's circular chorus, framed by a fierce guitar lick set in a thick mix of plush noises sets up the main course: an album that blends the band's veteran pop sensibility with the more adventurous helmsmanship of producer Don Smith (Cracker).

This combination of eccentric hooks and melody couldn't have been more unfashionable when the Rembrandts got together in 1990. "When we first started out, melody wasn't such a coveted thing on radio," says Phil Solem. "The trend was for more beat-oriented stuff. A lot of bands were tempted to change their style to fit radio's needs." He and his partner Danny Wilde stuck it out though, and were rewarded with the 1990 radio smash "That's Just The Way It Is Baby." The hit single, which came off their critically acclaimed debut album The Rembrandts, also brought a new dilemma for the two members. Was the group destined to be a hit-driven act, or would they be given time to nurture their "love of a good song" and establish themselves as songwriters. Getting snared in such a quandry can lead to some unusual projects. The new album features an example of the Rembrandts' versatility on "I'll Be There For You," the theme song from the Warner Bros. Television smash hit comedy series "FRIENDS." The producers for the Top Five show approached the group about singing the opening theme, and the duo obliged. The song has already become a cult classic of sorts, but the group wants to make sure that fans know the new album is as diverse as any previous Rembrandts offering.

"Even when we had the hit we were still fighting the 'leather jacket' thing that seemed to dominate MTV," says Danny. "There's always a flavor of the month. We'd be doing a disservice to ourselves if we didn't care about the songs." Both work-a-day musicians, Danny has his own studio in Los Angeles, California, and Phil holes up in Minnesota working there. "We'll write separately and then hook up here to record or polish the songs," says Phil. "On the song 'Lovin' Me Insane' we were just in the studio jamming. I came up with the riff which is sideways sounding, then we threw the 'insanity' thing in there. The song ended up being about a stalker and his victim." The song, which bounces along on a jig-saw series of chords, has an almost T-Rex feel to it. The band has long cited 60's and 70's influences as sparks in their musical engine. "We've always had an affection for stuff like the Beatles, and Bowie and the Yardbirds," says Danny.

The duo's affinity for the above mentioned music found them both hanging out in the L.A. music scene in the 1970's. "It was really decadent back then in the mid to late seventies. We had one band called Great Buildings," says Phil. "The band thing started wearing on us so I moved back to Minnesota but we kept in touch. We kept actively making music together and separately." The early eighties saw Danny make one solo album for Island records and two for Geffen. Keeping the faith in their songwriting ability sustained the two until they decided to become a band again. But this time they decided to record a demo, which eventually ended up being released 'as is' as The Rembrandts. With that success under their belt, the duo went on to produce their follow up album, 1992's Untitled, which included the Top 30 hit "Johnny Have You Seen Her." Feeling vindicated for sticking to their ideals, the two wry musicians approached the making of their current album with wisdom intact. "We wouldn't have careers right now if we jumped on every bandwagon we've watched roll by," laughs Danny. Phil seconds the notion. If the methodology of the Rembrandts has been to 'write from the heart', they're also seasoned enough to know that 'pulling it off' is what makes a song really great. Strange things often happen between the conception of a song and the track that's finally produced. "That's what was so great about working with Don Smith. He's not just a knob-turner," says Phil. It's taken years for Danny and Phil to know just what threads to pull on to keep that kind of tension without the whole thing unraveling. Add to the mix engineer Gavin MacKillop (his credits include producing Toad The Wet Sprocket) and Don Smith's aural compass (he engineered the Stone's VooDoo Lounge LP for Producer Don Was) and you've got the cagiest Rembrandts album yet.

"We did the first album in my garage," reminisces Danny. "Our goal is to continue to capture that fresh and simple approach to our recordings. No matter how much you 'know' about making records, it's doing it that keeps the fire going."

On the Rembrandts' third effort, LP, the oil burned was well worth it.

© 1995 EastWest Records America